DAVID EDGAR

David Edgar was born in 1948 into a theatre family. After a period in journalism, he took up writing full time in 1972. He founded and directed Britain's first post-graduate course in playwriting studies, at the University of Birmingham, from 1989 to 1999.

His previous plays for the National Theatre are the 1987 promenade play *Entertaining Strangers* (a new version of a community play for Dorchester, directed by Peter Hall) and *The Shape of the Table* (1990). For the Royal Shakespeare Company, he wrote *Destiny* (1976, winner of the Arts Council's John Whiting award); *Maydays* (1983, winner of the Plays and Players award) and *Pentecost* (1994-5, winner of the Evening Standard best play award); as well as adaptations of *The Jail Diary of Albie Sachs*, *Dr Jekyll and Mr Hyde* and *Nicholas Nickleby* (directed by Trevor Nunn and John Caird, and winner of the Society of West End Theatre and New York Tony best play awards). His other stage work includes *O Fair Jerusalem* (Birmingham Repertory Theatre, 1975), *Saigon Rose* (Traverse Theatre, Edinburgh, 1976), *Mary Barnes* (Birmingham Repertory Theatre, then the Royal Court, 1978-9), and *That Summer* (Hampstead Theatre, 1987).

David Edgar has also written several plays for the BBC, including the three-part serial *Vote for Them* (with Neil Grant, BBC2, 1989); *A Movie Starring Me* (Radio 4, 1991); *Buying a Landslide* (BBC2, 1992); *Talking to Mars* (Radio 3, 1996) and a dramatisation of Eve Brook's *The Secret Parts* (Radio 4, 2000). He wrote the biographical *Citizen Locke* for Channel 4 (1994) and the film *Lady Jane*, directed by Trevor Nunn for Paramount (1986). His libretto *The Bridge* (written for the Stephen Oliver prize in 1996 and set by Tim Benjamin) was performed at the Northern College of Music and as part of the Covent Garden Festival in 1998.

David Edgar writes and reviews for a wide variety of journals. A collection of his non-dramatic writings, *The Second Time as Farce*, was published by Lawrence and Wishart in 1988. He edited and introduced a book of contributions to the Birmingham Theatre Conference, *State of Play*, in 1999.

By the same author

Destiny

Entertaining Strangers

The Jail Diary of Albie Sachs

Mary Barnes

Nicholas Nickleby

Pentecost

Teendreams & Our Own People

That Summer

The Shape of the Table

Wreckers

Vote for Them

Edgar Plays: One (*Destiny, Mary Barnes, The Jail Diary of Albie Sachs, Saigon Rose, O Fair Jerusalem*)

Edgar Plays: Two (*Ecclesiastes, Nicholas Nickleby, Entertaining Strangers*)

Edgar Plays: Three (*Our Own People, Teendreams, Maydays, That Summer*)

Edgar: Shorts (*Blood Sports* with *Ball Boys, Baby Love, The National Theatre, The Midas Connection*)

The Second Time as Farce

State of Play (*editor and introduction*)

DAVID EDGAR

Albert Speer

based on the book
Albert Speer: His Battle with Truth
by Gitta Sereny

NICK HERN BOOKS
London
www.nickhernbooks.co.uk

A Nick Hern Book

Albert Speer, based on the book *Albert Speer: His Battle with Truth*
by Gitta Sereny, first published in Great Britain as a paperback original
in 2000 by Nick Hern Books Ltd, 14 Larden Road, London W3 7ST

Albert Speer copyright © David Edgar 2000

'Afterword' © David Edgar, 2000

'Principal Characters' and 'Chronology of the Third Reich'
copyright © Royal National Theatre 2000, printed with permission

Front cover design: courtesy Michael Mayhew

Typeset by Country Setting, Kingsdown, Kent CT14 8ES

Printed by Biddles, Guildford

A CIP catalogue record for this book is available from the British Library

ISBN 1 85459 485 0

David Edgar has asserted his right to be identified as the
author of this work

Albert Speer: His Battle with Truth by Gitta Sereny first published
in Great Britain in 1995 by Macmillan, published in paperback
by Picador in 1996

To Stephanie

Contents

AUTHOR'S NOTE

Gitta Sereny's *Albert Speer: His Battle with Truth* is a 720-page book, written with the utmost historical rigour, about a man whose long life was dominated by the defining event of the twentieth century. In order to write a stage play based on this work I have had to conflate characters, combine scenes and concentrate the incidents on which they are based.

As ever, the aim of this is better to reveal the truth. This is a vulnerable procedure in a play based on a biography in which the truth is pursued but also questioned. I am hugely grateful for the chance to retell the story Gitta Sereny has told so authoritatively in her book. For the consequences of doing so in a very different medium, I am responsible.

In addition to Gitta Sereny herself, I am indebted to Michael Eaton and Hilary Norrish for their contribution to the shape and content of the play as it developed through treatment into draft. As with our earlier stage collaboration, *Nicholas Nickleby*, Trevor Nunn had an immense influence on the structure, substance and meaning of the text, both before and during rehearsals.

Finally, two practical notes. In order to counter the notion that Nazism could only have happened in a foreign language, I've anglicised most of the ranks and titles in the play. The ones left in German are those for which an English translation is misleading: 'Führer' doesn't mean the same as 'Leader', 'Gauleiter' implies something different from 'Governor', and while 'Herr' does mean 'Mr' it is often used in conjunction with other titles in a way which sounds odd to an English ear. Second, where lines are broken in the text, I have indicated the point at which the next character interrupts by a slash. The rest of the first character's line does not have to be completed: it is there to provide some overlap but also to indicate to the actor where the interrupted sentence was going.

David Edgar, May 2000

Albert Speer by David Edgar, based on Gitta Sereny's book
Albert Speer: His Battle with Truth, was first performed in the
Lyttelton at the National Theatre on 16 May 2000. Press night
was 25 May.The cast, in order of appearance, was:

Albert Speer	Alex Jennings
Nuremberg Prosecutor	William Gaunt
Nuremberg Judge	John Nolan

Spandau Prison, 1947

French Officer	Patrick Baladi
Russian Director	Charles Millham
Guard	Stephen Ballantyne
Soviet Guard	Patrick Marlowe
Konstantin von Neurath, foreign minister	Pip Donaghy
Admiral Karl Dönitz	Martin Chamberlain
Baldur von Schirach, Hitler Youth leader	David Weston
Rudolf Hess, Hitler's Deputy	Sylvester Morand
Walther Funk, economics minister	Iain Mitchell
Admiral Erich Raeder	Benny Young
Georges Casalis, Calvinist pastor	Jonathan Cullen

Germany and the Occupied Territories, 1931–45

Rudolf Wolters, architect	Simon Day
Hans Tessenow, architect	Pip Donaghy
Architecture students	Patrick Baladi, Stephen Ballantyne, Giles Smith, Chris Vance
Adolf Hitler	Roger Allam
Colonel Nicolas von Below, adjutant	Adrian Penketh
Karl Hanke, party official, later Gauleiter	Iain Mitchell
Margret Speer, Speer's wife	Jessica Turner

Anne-Marie Wittenberg (later Kempf), Speer's secretary

	Christine Kavanagh
Julius Schaub, adjutant	John Nolan
Dr Fritz Todt, Minister of Armaments	Pip Donaghy
Speer's Father	William Gaunt
Frau Maria von Below	Imogen Slaughter
Eva Braun	Cathryn Bradshaw
Frau Anni Brandt	Tilly Blackwood
First Adjutant	Stephen Ballantyne
Fräulein Johanna Wolf, secretary	Sally Ann Burnett
Second Adjutant	Charles Millham
Fräulein Christa Schröder, secretary	Elizabeth Conboy
Theodor Ganzenmüller, railway official	Patrick Baladi
Major in Ukraine	Benny Young
Ukrainian Tufties	Chloe Angharad, Sally-Ann Burnett, Elizabeth Conboy, Imogen Slaughter
Speer Construction Workers	Martin Chamberlain, Patrick Marlowe, Giles Smith, Chris Vance
State Secretary, Ministry of Armaments	John Nolan
His Assistant	David Weston
Ernst, Speer's brother	Stephen Ballantyne
Dr Professor Friedrich Koch	David Weston
Heinrich Himmler, Reichsführer-SS	Benny Young

Germany and England, 1966–81

Hans Flachsner, Speer's lawyer	David Weston
Pressmen	Martin Chamberlain, Charles Millham, John Nolan, David Weston, Chris Vance, Benny Young
Heckler	Iain Mitchell
Albert, Speer's son	Stephen Ballantyne
Hilde Schramm, Speer's daughter	Cathryn Bradshaw
Ulf Schramm, her husband	Iain Mitchell
Ruth, Albert's wife	Sally Ann Burnett
Arnold, Speer's son	Chris Vance
Fritz, Speer's son	Giles Smith
Margret Nissen, Speer's daughter	Elizabeth Conboy
Hans Nissen, her husband	Adrian Penketh
Ernst, Speer's son	Patrick Marlowe
Waitresses	Chloe Angharad, Imogen Slaughter

Wolf-Jobst Siedler, Speer's publisher   William Gaunt
Mrs Winteringham   Tilly Blackwood
Publishers   Elizabeth Conboy, Charles Millham
Chair of University Meeting   Sally-Ann Burnett
Hecklers   Stephen Ballantyne, Chris Vance, David Weston
Questioners   Patrick Marlowe, Elizabeth Conboy,
John Nolan, Martin Chamberlain, Benny Young
Robert Raphael Geis, Rabbi   Pip Donaghy
David, his assistant   Patrick Baladi
Hotel Waiter   Patrick Marlowe

Director Trevor Nunn
Set Designer Ian MacNeil
Costume Designer Joan Wadge
Lighting Designer Rick Fisher
Video Design Chris Laing
Music Steven Edis
Movement Director Kate Flatt
Sound Designer Chris Shutt
Company Voice Work Patsy Rodenburg
Associate Set Designer Paul Atkinson

ALBERT SPEER

O, would that I had never seen Wittenberg,
never read book! and what wonders I have done,
all Germany can witness, yea, all the world;
for which Faustus has lost both Germany and the world,
and must remain in hell for ever.

Christopher Marlowe, *Dr Faustus*, last scene

For the commission to do a great building,
I would have sold my soul like Faust.
Now I had found my Mephistopheles.
He seemed no less engaging than Goethe's.

Albert Speer, *Inside the Third Reich*

CHARACTERS

Albert SPEER

Nuremberg PROSECUTOR
Nuremberg JUDGE

Spandau Prison, 1947

FRENCH OFFICER
RUSSIAN DIRECTOR
GUARD
SOVIET GUARD
Konstantin von NEURATH, foreign minister
Admiral Karl DÖNITZ
Baldur von SCHIRACH, Hitler Youth leader
Rudolf HESS, Hitler's Deputy
Walther FUNK, economics minister
Admiral Erich RAEDER
Georges CASALIS, Calvinist pastor

Germany and the Occupied Territories, 1931–45

Rudolf WOLTERS, architect
Hans TESSENOW, architect
Adolf HITLER
Karl HANKE, party official, later Gauleiter
MARGRET Speer, Speer's wife
ANNEMARIE Wittenberg (later Kempf), Speer's secretary
Colonel Nicolas VON BELOW, adjutant
Julius SCHAUB, adjutant
Dr Fritz TODT, Minister of Armaments
Speer's FATHER
FRAU Maria VON BELOW
EVA BRAUN

FRAU Anni BRANDT
Two young ADJUTANTS (at the Berghof)
FRÄULEIN Johanna WOLF, secretary
FRÄULEIN Christa SCHRÖDER, secretary
Theodor GANZENMÜLLER, railway official
MAJOR in Ukraine
Six members SPEER construction SQUAD
STATE SECRETARY, Ministry of Armaments
His ASSISTANT
ERNST, Speer's brother
DR Professor Friedrich KOCH
Heinrich HIMMLER, Reichsführer-SS

Germany and England, 1966–81

Hans FLACHSNER, Speer's lawyer
ALBERT, Speer's son
HILDE Schramm, Speer's daughter
ULF Schramm, her husband
RUTH, Albert's wife
ARNOLD, Speer's son
FRITZ, Speer's son
MARGRET (JNR) Nissen, Speer's daughter
HANS Nissen, her husband
ERNST (JNR), Speer's son
Wolf-Jobst SIEDLER, Speer's publisher
MRS WINTERINGHAM
Young PUBLISHERS
CHAIR of University Meeting
Two HECKLERS
Five QUESTIONERS
Robert Raphael GEIS, Rabbi
DAVID, his assistant

Architecture Students, Ukrainian Tufties, Staff Officers,
Adjutants, Pressmen and Hecklers, Publishers and Partygoers,
Audience at University Meeting

ACT ONE

'For five years I lived in this world of plans,
and in spite of all their defects and absurdities
I still cannot entirely tear myself away from it all'.

Albert Speer, *Inside the Third Reich*

ACT ONE

1.1.1   Heidelberg, 1970s

Around 70 years old, ALBERT SPEER *sits in a chair, sleeping and dreaming. He remembers the charges and sentences passed at the Nuremberg trial of the Nazi leaders.*

PROSECUTOR. The Defendant Speer – between 1932 and 1945 was: A member of the Nazi Party, Reichsleiter, member of the Reichstag, Reich Minister for Armaments and Munitions, \ Chief of the Organization Todt, General Plenipotentiary for Armaments in the Office of the Four Year Plan, and Chairman of the Armaments Council.

JUDGE. In accordance with Article 27 of the Charter, the International Military Tribunal will now pronounce the sentences on the defendants convicted in this indictment. Defendant Joachim von Ribbentrop, on the counts of the indictment on which you have been convicted, the Tribunal sentences you to death by hanging. Defendant Ernst Kaltenbrunner, the Tribunal sentences you to death by hanging.

PROSECUTOR. The defendant Speer used the foregoing positions and his personal influence in such a manner that: \ He participated in the military and economic planning and preparation of the Nazi conspirators for Wars of aggression and Wars in Violation of International Treaties, Agreements, and Assurances set forth in Count One and Count Two of the Indictment . . .

JUDGE. Defendant Julius Streicher, the Tribunal sentences you to death by hanging.

PROSECUTOR. . . . and he authorized, directed, and participated in the War Crimes set forth in Count Three of the Indictment . . .

JUDGE. Defendant Fritz Sauckel, the Tribunal sentences you to death by hanging.

PROSECUTOR. . . . and the Crimes against Humanity set forth in Count Four of the Indictment, including more particularly the abuse and exploitation of human beings for forced labour in the conduct of aggressive war.

JUDGE. Defendant Albert Speer! On the counts of the indictment on which you have been convicted, the Tribunal sentences you to death by hanging!

SPEER *wakes in terrible agitation.*

SPEER. Not – yet.

1.2.1   Spandau, 18 July 1947

The RUSSIAN DIRECTOR *and a* FRENCH OFFICER *and* GUARDS *await prisoners in a reception hall in Spandau prison. Seven concentration camp uniforms set out. A door opens and a* GUARD *admits Konstantin von* NEURATH, *wearing shabby civilian clothes.*

RUSSIAN DIRECTOR (*from a list, to* NEURATH, *emphatically, but with terrible pronunciation*). Konstantin von Neurath. Foreign Minister. Fifteen year.

FRENCH OFFICER. On admission, the prisoners will undress completely. Prisoners will be addressed by their convict number, in no circumstances by name.

RUSSIAN DIRECTOR. Now you are Number one.

NEURATH *undresses.* KARL DÖNITZ *is admitted.*

Grand Admiral Karl Dönitz: ten year. Number Two.

DÖNITZ *undresses. Baldur von* SCHIRACH *is admitted.*

Baldur von Schirach. Hitler youth leader, twenty year. Number Three.

SCHIRACH *undresses.* HESS *is admitted.*

RUSSIAN DIRECTOR. Ah. Hess. Hitler Deputy, till 1941. Sentence to life. Is number four.

HESS *doesn't undress.* SPEER *admitted. He is 42.*

RUSSIAN DIRECTOR. Albert Speer, Arm Minister, 20 year.

SPEER *sizes up the situation.*

RUSSIAN DIRECTOR. I say a lucky man.

GUARD (*shouts to* HESS). Undress!

RUSSIAN DIRECTOR. His number five.

HESS *and* SPEER *begin to undress. We sense hostility from the other* PRISONERS *to* SPEER. *Walter* FUNK *is admitted.*

RUSSIAN DIRECTOR (*to* FUNK *and* RAEDER). Walter Funk, Reichsminister for Economics. Number six, for life.

Erich RAEDER *is admitted.*

And Admiral Erich Raeder is number seven. Also life.

As the later PRISONERS *finish undressing, the* FRENCH OFFICER *continues to read out the rules.* GUARDS *gesture to them to go and dress in the concentration camp uniforms.* HESS *is swaying.*

FRENCH OFFICER. The discipline of the institution requires that prisoners should adopt a standing position whenever approached or in the presence of prison officers. They will salute by standing at attention at the same time removing their headgear.

HESS *gestures to the* GUARD *who goes to speak to him. A* GUARD *goes and whispers to him.*

The prisoners may approach an officer or warder only if ordered to do so or if they want to make a request.

RUSSIAN DIRECTOR (*in Russian*). Ftchyom tam dela? [What's the problem?]

GUARD (*nodding to* HESS). This man says he will faint.

RUSSIAN DIRECTOR (*Russian*). Poost syadit. [Let him sit down.]

GUARD (*to* HESS). You must sit down.

HESS *sits on the floor. The other* PRISONERS *continue to dress.*

FRENCH OFFICER (*continues*). Prisoners shall at all times wear the clothing provided for them. Imprisonment shall be in the form of solitary confinement. Approaching any window – including those in the cells – is strictly prohibited. The Prisoners may not talk or associate with one another except with special dispensation from the Directorate. However religious services and walks in open air will be carried out together.

RUSSIAN DIRECTOR. Form line!

The PRISONERS *form up in their concentration camp uniforms.*

RUSSIAN DIRECTOR (*Russian*). Zaklyutchyonnym vazzmozhina boodit intiressna oozznat shto etoo adezhdoo nasseeli oozniki konstlagirey. [The Prisoners may be interested to learn that these clothes were worn by prisoners in concentration camps.]

GUARD (*translates*). The Prisoners must like to know that these cloths are worn by prisoners in concentration camp.

No response from the PRISONERS.

RUSSIAN DIRECTOR (*Russian*). Im shto, ni panyatna? [Do they understand that?]

GUARD (*translates*). Do you understand?

The PRISONERS *give slight nods.* HESS *nods and is helped to his feet.*

RUSSIAN OFFICER. So, gentlemen. Welcome to Spandau.

As the DIRECTOR, OFFICER, GUARDS *and* PRISONERS *leave, and the next scene is set up,* SPEER *speaks out front.*

SPEER. You ask me how I felt? That I was getting what I
deserved.

What, did I really feel that? Well, my feelings then were
complex. I am putting them in simple terms for you.

But I can assure you, at that moment, nothing could have
been better designed to make me feel very humble indeed.

1.2.2   Spandau, October 1947

GEORGES CASALIS *has come in to a double cell which has
been appointed for use as a chapel. He carries a suitcase.
There is one table and the cell lavatory.* CASALIS, *a young
Calvinist pastor, opens the case, takes out a wooden cross and
places it on the table. He takes out a Bible and finds himself a
black cassock. He takes off his jacket and is putting the cassock
on when he hears the rumble of an approaching congregation.*

He hurries to finish dressing as a SOVIET GUARD *leads in*
RAEDER, FUNK, DÖNITZ, SCHIRACH, NEURATH *and*
SPEER, *dragging chairs. There is a moment when the* SOVIET
GUARD *and the* SIX PRISONERS *stand watching a* YOUNG
MAN *having a fight with his cassock.* CASALIS *wins, looks
round for someone he recognises and holds out his hand to*
DÖNITZ.

CASALIS. Herr Dönitz.

After a moment, DÖNITZ *puts his chair upright and shakes*
CASALIS's *hand.*

(*To the next man.*) Herr Schirach?

SCHIRACH. Yes.

Shake hands.

CASALIS (*to* FUNK). And – Raeder?

FUNK. Funk.

CASALIS. Herr Funk.

FUNK (*shaking hands, nodding to the next man*). Raeder.

RAEDER. Admiral Raeder.

CASALIS (*shaking hands*). How do you do. And . . . Herr von Neurath.

> NEURATH *shakes, pleased that* CASALIS *used the 'von'.*

And of course, Herr . . .

SPEER. Speer.

CASALIS. Herr Speer.

> *Shakes hands. To the* GUARD.

Herr Hess?

> *The* GUARD *is baffled.*

NEURATH (*Russian*). Nommerr chetyrree. [Number Four.]

SOVIET GUARD. He is in cell. No religion. 'Mumbo jumbo'.

> *He indicates by the universal gesture that* HESS *is mad.*

CASALIS. Please gentlemen be seated.

> *The* PRISONERS *sit on their chairs. The* SOVIET GUARD *sits on the lavatory.*

My name is Georges Casalis. I minister to the Protestant French community here in Berlin. I was asked if I would be prepared to serve as pastor to the prisoners of Spandau, on the grounds I fear of my linguistic rather than my spiritual skills.

> *No laugh.*

So, as required of me: your regular Saturday dose of mumbo jumbo.

> *No laugh.*

The text on which I wish to speak today is taken from Luke's gospel: 'While he was in a certain city, there came a man full of leprosy – '

The PRISONERS *glance at each other.*

' – and when he saw Jesus he fell on his face and begged him: Lord, if you will, make me clean.'

SCHIRACH *a bark of a laugh.* DÖNITZ *leans over and whispers to* FUNK.

Now, you may ask, why I have chosen this passage to discuss with you today.

The PRISONERS *are chuntering.* CASALIS *looks up from his notes, deciding to confront the atmosphere directly.*

But before I say anything more to you, I sense that you have something you want to say to me.

RAEDER *stands. The* SOVIET GUARD *stands too.*

RAEDER. Herr Pastor, we must protest.

CASALIS. Uh – why?

RAEDER. It is entirely inappropriate to address us in this way.

CASALIS. In what \ way?

FUNK. As lepers.

CASALIS. Ah.

Slight pause. SCHIRACH *stands.*

SCHIRACH. We are here not as criminals, but because we have been unjustly condemned.

DÖNITZ (*stands*). As men who only did their military duty.

FUNK (*stands*). Therefore we protest, in the strongest possible terms.

RAEDER. And if our protest should prove ineffective –

NEURATH. – we shall take official action.

A moment of standoff. NEURATH *stands.* SPEER *stands.*

CASALIS. Gentlemen –

DÖNITZ. And so good morning, Herr Pastor.

DÖNITZ *leads the group, picking up their chairs and dragging them to the exit.*

SOVIET GUARD. You want be take to cell?

DÖNITZ. 'We want be take to cell'.

SPEER *is following the group.*

CASALIS. But gentlemen –

The GUARD *calls up the corridor to other* GUARDS.

SOVIET GUARD (*in Russian*). Kapitan Razzinskiy! Mne noozhna vasha pomashch! Dvaa tchelaveka! [Captain Rozinsky! I need your help! Two men!]

CASALIS. But, gentlemen, I don't know what to do.

The PRISONERS *look back at him, a little contemptuously.*

If the words of the Bible are an offence to you, how can I be of help?

The other GUARDS *arrive.*

I had hoped we were to set out on a journey, to find common ground between us and our inner selves. Tomorrow, I shall deliver the sermon I have not delivered here, to my own congregation. Next week I planned to speak to you and then to them from Mark: 'Those who are well have no need of a physician'.

He puts the Bible and the cross in the suitcase, and slams it shut.

That is, to anyone who wants to hear me.

RAEDER. We shall see.

DÖNITZ *leads the* PRISONERS *out.* SPEER *lingers. When the others have gone, the* SOVIET GUARD *gestures for him to follow.* SPEER *demurs.* CASALIS *is picking up his suitcase.*

SPEER. Well, that put the cat among the pigeons.

CASALIS *realises that* SPEER *wants to speak to him. He puts down his suitcase.*

CASALIS. That was not of course \ my intention –

SPEER. You should however pay no attention to that little
   spectacle.

CASALIS. I fear \ that's not as easy –

SPEER. Your sermons *should* upset us. You should not spare
   anybody's feelings.

CASALIS. No. Well, thank you.

   Pause.

   Herr Speer, would you like to join your comrades?

SPEER. Oh, come now, Herr Pastor. You have done your
   homework. You know that even if I saw those gentlemen
   as comrades, they would hardly think that way of me.

   Pause.

CASALIS (*to* GUARD). Please, leave us for a moment.

   After a beat, the GUARD *understands, and leaves, shutting
   and locking the door behind him.*

   Your defence at Nuremberg: Your position in the government
   was merely technical. You made no ideological statements.
   You were aware that people were evacuated but you had no
   idea that they were being systematically put to death.

SPEER. But nevertheless . . .

CASALIS. Nevertheless it was your duty to assume your share
   of the responsibility for the catastrophe of the world war.
   Insofar as Hitler gave you orders and you obeyed them you
   must share the blame.

SPEER. Well done.

CASALIS (*aware of being patronised*). Well, thank you.

SPEER. So it will be no surprise that number five is hardly
   number one in the affections of his fellow-prisoners.

CASALIS. No.

SPEER. In the same way as I would imagine you are hardly
   popular with your associates.

CASALIS. I beg your pardon?

SPEER. I wondered what your comrades in the French Resistance think about your present ministry?

CASALIS. You've done your homework too.

SPEER *acknowledges with a gesture.*

I think they are suspicious of its premise.

SPEER *looks questioningly.*

Which is, that the greatest sinner can repent. And now Herr Speer, I think you should tell me what you want to say or go back to your cell.

Pause.

SPEER. I want to know if they are right. You spoke about a journey to becoming someone else. I wondered if you felt that anyone can leave their past behind, and become a different man. Or if there are crimes – and criminals – so terrible there is no price too high for them to pay.

CASALIS. What is the past self that you want to leave behind?

SPEER. The man who thinks it's possible to be merely technical.

CASALIS. And what price do you think your crimes deserve?

SPEER. That is the question.

Slight pause.

CASALIS. Herr Speer. I don't think I am looking at a man who wished he'd died at Nuremberg.

SPEER *looks questioning.*

But perhaps . . . a man who thinks he ought to have wanted to die.

Slight pause.

And yes. The crimes for which you took responsibility were terrible. In the scale of justice, maybe, for a judge, a jury, yes, there is no price too high. But I am not a lawyer, I am not here to judge, to probe or to interrogate. I am a priest, and as such I am not concerned with balancing your suffering against the suffering for which you were undoubtedly responsible. All I see before me is an individual soul. Alone, alive, and thus, yes, capable of change.

SPEER. And is this a journey I must make alone?

Pause.

CASALIS. Not if you'd prefer to walk in company.

Slight pause.

But only if you tell the truth, to me and to yourself. For although it's possible that a man be born again, to do so he must confront the truth of what he was before.

1.3.1   Germany, 1920s

SPEER *out front:*

SPEER. And so I tried to do so. Starting with my childhood, how at school I shone at mathematics, how my father nevertheless persuaded me to follow him into an architectural career. And how despite, yes, some initial disappointment, this course of study took me from provincial Heidelberg to Munich, to new interests and new friends.

Enter RUDOLF WOLTERS, *a couple of years older than* SPEER, *now in his 20s. He tosses* SPEER *his informal 1930s clothes, into which* SPEER *changes, as:*

WOLTERS. Say, you know your problem, Albert? You don't do any work, you dress like a tramp, you're always late and you can't draw. Correct those faults, and you might make something of yourself in architecture.

SPEER (*to* CASALIS). Which of course was absolutely \ true.

WOLTERS. Oh, and that's not to mention spending all your time with girls far too pretty for you doing pointlessly exhausting things in boats, down rivers and up mountains.

SPEER. Which was also true. The woman, naturally, was to become my wife. But this was after I had followed Rudi Wolters to the capital, falling under the influence of the great Heinrich Tessenow . . .

WOLTERS. . . . whose deep knowledge of the classical tradition . . .

SPEER. . . . love of peasant culture and hostility to internationalism . . .

WOLTERS. . . . inspires us all.

TESSENOW appears, bringing young ARCHITECTURE STUDENTS *in his wake.*

TESSENOW. So what is simple?

STUDENTS. Simple is not always good.

TESSENOW. But what is good?

STUDENTS. It's always simple.

TESSENOW. And where will we find good and simple?

STUDENTS. Not in the cities! With the peasants! In the countryside!

SPEER. He told us in his classes in Berlin.

TESSENOW. And so what three things unite the principles of Germanic peasant architecture with those of Agrigento, Paestum and the Parthenon?

The STUDENTS *are all keen to answer but* TESSENOW *silences them with a raised finger.*

Herr Speer?

SPEER. Simplicity.

SPEER *momentarily stumped.* WOLTERS *gestures at his own body.*

SPEER. The proportions of the human form. And um . . .

WOLTERS *holds up three fingers.*

The rule of three.

TESSENOW. Exactly and precisely and entirely so.

TESSENOW sweeps off, followed by the STUDENTS, *echoing:*

STUDENTS. Exactly and precisely and entirely so . . .

SPEER. But what changed my life and fortunes was a chance meeting with the head of my party district.

CASALIS. You are in the party now?

SPEER. Yes, I joined in 1931.

CASALIS. Two years before Hitler came to power.

SPEER. Yes.

CASALIS. You will understand that for me that needs some explanation.

SPEER. Oh, Herr Pastor, just the chaos and despair of the depression. The six million unemployed.

CASALIS. Of course. But, still . . .

SPEER. And a meeting I had been persuaded by my fellow students to attend.

Massive applause. YOUNG NAZIS *run in to catch a glimpse of a* MAN *in a blue suit, surrounded by an entourage of* MINDERS, *striding purposefully across the stage.* SPEER *finds himself caught up in their enthusiasm. Finally, the group rushes forward to the front of the stage, saluting and chanting:*

YOUNG NAZIS. Sieg heil! Sieg heil! Sieg heil!

On the last of which SPEER *finds himself joining in. The* YOUNG NAZIS *withdraw.*

CASALIS. And do you remember what he said?

SPEER. Well, as I recall, he concentrated on the way in which the war had eliminated the best, leaving the inferior in charge.

CASALIS. And what you felt?

SPEER. Well, I'd expected a vulgar rabble-rouser. In fact, he
seemed quite quiet, almost shy . . .

CASALIS. But what you *felt?*

Slight pause.

SPEER. I felt he was a human being. That here was somebody
who cared for us, the young. Who loved us. Individually.
And afterwards I drove into the country, to the woods. And
walked all night. And joined the Party.

And as the only member of my section with a car, and thus
perforce a member of the Party's motorists' association,
I was immediately appointed section head, and thus came
to the notice of Karl Hanke, then a rising star.

1.3.2   Railway Station, Berlin, July 1932

KARL HANKE *enters in party uniform. Also* SPEER*'s wife*
MARGRET, *with a* PORTER, *and the luggage of a boating
holiday – collapsible boats and all – on his trolley.*

HANKE. Speer.

SPEER. Who one day in 1932 pursued me to the Lehrter
railway station.

HANKE. Thank God I've found you. They told me at your
lodgings you had gone away.

SPEER. That's right, I have. On Holiday.

MARGRET *approaches.*

MARGRET. Albert, the train is leaving.

HANKE. On holiday? For Christ's sake, where?

SPEER. East Prussia. We're going faltboating.

MARGRET. In fact, in less than five \ minutes –

HANKE. And all this – stuff –

SPEER. Is our equipment. My dear, this is Party Comrade Hanke.

MARGRET. I am very pleased \ to meet you.

HANKE. But Speer you cannot possibly . . . You know that we have taken over premises in the Voss Strasse?

SPEER. Yes.

HANKE. Which the Doctor wishes to refurbish. Instantly.

SPEER. Uh – yes?

HANKE. Speer, you claimed you were an architect.

SPEER. I am.

A whistle blows.

MARGRET. Um, Albert –

SPEER. And yes of course I will.

HANKE. Good man, good man. Thank God.

HANKE *goes out.* SPEER *looks at* MARGRET *and the luggage.*

MARGRET. The Doctor?

SPEER. Goebbels.

MARGRET. Ah. So we don't go on holiday.

MARGRET *goes out with the luggage.*

CASALIS. So, effectively, your career began with Goebbels.

SPEER. And continued with him, yes.

1.3.3   Voss Strasse, Berlin, July 1932

ANNEMARIE WITTENBERG *appears, carrying files and office equipment. She is 18.*

ANNEMARIE. Herr Speer. My name is Annemarie Wittenberg.

SPEER. How do you do?

ANNEMARIE. You are the man who painted the outer office red?

SPEER. That's right.

ANNEMARIE. And Party Comrade Hanke's office yellow?

SPEER. Yes.

ANNEMARIE. I work in Dr Goebbels' office. I am very happy there. But now, apparently, I have to work for you.

She goes out.

SPEER. And then in 1933, I saw some drawings on Karl Hanke's desk.

1.3.4 Voss Strasse, Berlin, April 1933

Enter HANKE *with design drawings.*

HANKE. What are you saying? This appears to be 'The backdrop for "a shooting match"?'

SPEER. Well, I said, the decoration for a rifle meeting. Not for a May Day rally to be addressed by the Chancellor of Germany.

HANKE (*looking at another design*). And you think that this is better. Just these . . . three big flags.

SPEER. Well, they are are tall. But like the pillars of the Parthenon, they are proportionate.

HANKE *hands him the drawings.*

HANKE. Well, then. Why not.

HANKE *goes out.*

SPEER (*out front*). And I have to say that the effect was considered something of a triumph.

We see the flags.

So much so, that Goebbels claimed it as his own idea. And when the time came to design the annual party rally at Nuremberg in 1933, I was called to Munich.

1.3.5 Munich, June 1933

Enter HESS, *now 39, who takes the drawings from* SPEER *and looks at them.*

HESS. It is an eagle.

SPEER. Yes.

HESS. Around 20 metres wide?

SPEER. That's right. Of course . . .

HESS. And mounted . . .

SPEER. On a truss. With nails.

HESS. Just like a butterfly.

SPEER. The idea is to overwhelm the viewer with its power and strength.

HESS. Hm. Only the Führer can decide if this will do.

A decision.

You will go and see him. He is here in Munich, in his apartment on the Prinzregentenstrasse. That will do.

HESS *gives* SPEER *back the drawings and goes out. We see a* MAN's *back, sitting at a desk.* SPEER *approaches him.*

SPEER (*to* CASALIS). And so there he was. Sitting, looking at a pistol he'd dismantled on his desk. He didn't look up once. I put the drawing down, he looked it, and said:

HITLER. Agreed.

And now we see the great eagle too.

CASALIS. And that was it? How did you feel?

SPEER. I felt – well, maybe, just a little disappointed. But he was the Chancellor of Germany. And then having finished Goebbels' flat in record time, I was asked to join the team rebuilding the Chancellor's apartments. Out of which arose an incident which was far from disappointing.

1.4.1   Chancellory apartments, Berlin, October 1933

SPEER *goes out as* HITLER *enters, at speed, followed by his adjutant Julius* SCHAUB *and other* AIDES. SCHAUB *is 35, currently a Sergeant, though he will rise to General by 1945 without substantially changing his role. There could be painters and plasterers at work.*

HITLER. When is this happening? I was assured that this was happening. Ah. It has happened.

He looks upwards.

Yesterday this room had not been plastered. Now it has. The ceiling moulding's very handsome.

ANNEMARIE *and* WOLTERS *rush in.*

And the windows? When will they be glazed?

WOLTERS (*looking in panic at a sheaf of worknotes*). Um – I . . . I believe that they are due . . .

SPEER *enters in a hurry. He now wears a waistcoat, collar and tie. He has a large plaster mark on his coat.*

ANNEMARIE (*prompting*). The windows.

SPEER. Yes. The glazing in this section will begin on Friday.

HITLER. Will *begin*?

SPEER. And will be completed.

HITLER. And is the work on schedule, as a whole?

SPEER. It is.

Pause.

HITLER. I am in a hurry. All I have now are the state secretary's apartments. How am I supposed to invite anybody there? It's ridiculous how penny-pinching the Republic was. The entrance! And the elevator!

Slight pause. Suddenly, looking straight at SPEER.

You say this will be done on time?

SPEER. Yes, my Führer.

HITLER. So many people tell me what I need's impossible.

SPEER. This is absolutely possible.

HITLER *looks piercingly at* SPEER.

HITLER. You are the man who refurbished Dr Goebbels' flat. And designed the flags for the May Day rally at the Tempelhof?

SPEER. Yes, my Führer. But here of course I am merely making sure that the work's completed in the timescale you have set.

HITLER. Of course. Well, you must come to lunch.

SPEER. Thank you my Führer. I look forward to it.

SPEER *gives a slight bow.* HITLER *works out* SPEER*'s mistake.*

HITLER. I meant, today.

SPEER*'s second thought is the plaster on his jacket. He can't stop looking down at it.*

Don't worry about that.

He turns and goes. SPEER *turns to his colleagues.*

WOLTERS. Who would have thought . . .

ANNEMARIE. Herr *Speer.*

SPEER. Well, I . . .

SCHAUB. Herr Speer, I think the Führer means that you should follow him.

SPEER. Ah. Right.

> SPEER *hurries out, followed by* SCHAUB, *into:*

1.4.2   Hitler's apartments

HITLER *has a blue jacket with a party badge pinned on to it.*
SPEER *hurries in.*

SPEER. I'm sorry, I \ didn't realise you intended –

HITLER. Now, do you think that this will do?

> *He hands* SPEER *the jacket.*

SPEER. But surely, this is \ your own special –

HITLER. Please.

> SPEER *hurries to change.*
>
> So tell me, how did you complete the Goebbels project by
> that deadline?

SPEER. Well, naturally, my team were all infused \ with
commitment to the task –

HITLER. – with National Socialist ardour. Naturally. And?

SPEER. And I persuaded them to work around the clock.

HITLER. But even so . . . ?

SPEER. I had to dry the plaster every night, with an industrial
fan I borrowed from a laundry.

HITLER. Then I have made the right decision.

> SPEER *has changed his jacket.* HITLER *looks fixedly into*
> SPEER*'s eyes. After a moment,* SPEER *turns away.*
>
> Or have I?
>
> SPEER *turns back, staring into* HITLER*'s eyes. Enter*
> SCHAUB, *allowing both* SPEER *and* HITLER *to break the*
> *stare.*

SCHAUB. Your guests await, my Führer.

HITLER. Good. Come, let me introduce you to the Merry Chancellor's Café.

> HITLER *hands* SCHAUB SPEER*'s old jacket and leads him out towards:*

1.4.3   Hitler's dining room in the Chancellory apartments

The LUNCH GUESTS *are standing, waiting for Hitler's arrival. They are all men, mostly in Party or military brown: they include* DÖNITZ, SCHIRACH, *the elegant and patrician Colonel Nicolas* VON BELOW *(25) and the bull-necked and balding Dr Fritz* TODT *(44). They could also include* NEURATH *and* FUNK. HITLER *comes in,* SPEER *following. The conversation dries up as* HITLER *quickly works the room.*

HITLER. Party Comrade Schirach.

SCHIRACH. Heil, my Führer.

HITLER. Dr Todt.

TODT. My Führer.

HITLER (*to* DÖNITZ). Admiral.

> *Enter* HESS, *clearly late. He sees* SPEER *standing nervously on the edge of things, in Hitler's jacket.*

HITLER (*to von* BELOW). Colonel.

VON BELOW. Führer.

HESS. Speer what are you wearing?

> EVERYONE *turns and looks.*

Speer, this will not do. That is the Führer's party badge!

HITLER. Yes, and the Führer's jacket too. Herr Speer's was soiled in his morning's work.

HESS. My Führer, I apologise for lateness.

HITLER, *going to his place at the table:*

HITLER. No matter. No doubt you had last minute orders for your 'special cook'.

Laughter.

I have the best vegetarian chef in Germany.

He sits. Others sitting. SPEER *doesn't know where to go.*

And yet here I am . . . surrounded by eaters of burnt carrion! Herr Speer, please, sit by me.

After a moment, SPEER *hurries over to sit by* HITLER, *who turns to* HESS.

Now, Hess, you know Herr Speer.

HESS. I do.

HITLER. He refurbished Dr Goebbels' rooms in record time. And he conceived the podium display at the May Day rally.

HESS. Not to mention the eagle design at Nuremberg.

HITLER. Ah.

SPEER. Indeed, my Führer, you did me the honour of approving my design in person.

HITLER *looks to* SPEER, *a little surprised. Then he turns back to the company.*

HITLER. I am asked why I am so concerned with beauty, and I answer with a question.

Slight pause. No one likes to volunteer the question.

It is this. How could the great betrayal have occurred, in 1918, quite so quickly, so dramatically?

Slight pause.

And the answer is, as I have said a thousand times, that the best of Germany had been destroyed, shot to blazes by French niggers in the trenches. So but the weakest elements remained. Leaderless, feminised, and naturally prey to any revolutionary bacillus Jewish agitators might care to spread among them. That is why our only duty is to purge the nation of this pestilence, to pass on a healthy Germany to future generations. That is why I surround myself with young men who are passionately committed to the pure and to the beautiful. Those for whom the word 'impossible' does not exist!

He turns to SPEER, *gazing into his eyes.*

Of course. I remember you exactly.

1.4.4   Berlin, April 1934

The lunch party disappears. SPEER *breaks forward, to* CASALIS, *handing* HITLER*'s jacket to* SCHAUB:

SPEER. So do you see? Do you understand? At the age of 28, to be plucked from nothing, to be chosen as the brightest and the best of my profession, by the man who as we saw it was the saviour of Germany.

CASALIS. 'Saviour'. 'Chosen'.

SPEER. Yes.

A social affair. Enter HANKE *with* MARGRET *in formal dress.* HANKE *hands* SPEER *his jacket.*

HANKE. Well, go on, Speer. Now is the moment.

SPEER (*to* CASALIS). The privilege of being in his closest circle.

HANKE. Introduce her.

SPEER. And yes, the thrill of being close to power.

HITLER *comes over.*

HITLER. Speer. You are able to grace us with your presence. Can this mean that we've run out of work for you?

SPEER. No of course not. Führer, may I present my wife?

HITLER. Your wife?

Slight pause.

HITLER. Of course. I am enchanted by the privilege of your acquaintance. Frau Speer, how do you do.

He kisses her hand.

MARGRET. I am very well, my Führer.

HITLER. A redoubled pleasure, being unaware for all these months of your existence.

MARGRET *flashes a look at* SPEER.

SPEER. Um I . . .

HITLER. You will forgive me, madam, if I ask how long . . . ?

MARGRET. Six years, my Führer.

HITLER. What? Six *years*?

SPEER. Um, I . . .

HITLER. And may I ask if there is any more concealment? Have you children?

MARGRET. No, my Führer, not as yet.

SPEER. In fact, my Führer, as it happens \ we are planning –

HITLER. What, six years married and no children? *Speer.*

Slight pause.

On this occasion I can hardly praise your prompt delivery.

EVERYONE *laughs.*

Frau Speer, your husband is going to make me buildings that will last a thousand years.

He looks at SPEER, *bows, turns and goes.* SPEER *turns to* CASALIS.

1.4.5   Spandau, 1947-1950

SPEER. And from then on, it was one task after another. Buildings. Pavilions. The Chancellory. And of course the party congresses.

CASALIS. The searchlights in the sky.

SPEER. The cathedral of light, as it was called.

Which emerges from the darkness behind SPEER.

Which served to dramatise the spectacle, while concealing the unattractive paunches of the party bureaucrats. It's funny, isn't it, that if anything, it will be these, dramatics, that I'll be remembered for?

CASALIS. Does that concern you?

SPEER. Do you think it should? Sometimes I feel quite stirred, that the most successful creation of my life is an immaterial phenomenon.

CASALIS. Well, I can understand that. Dealing also as I do with immaterial phenonema. What is not there, as well as what is there.

SPEER. What do you mean?

CASALIS. I mean that perhaps those searchlights concealed more than the bellies of the bureaucrats.

SPEER. In Nuremberg, they had psychologists. They showed us inkblots. We had to tell them the first thing that we thought of.

CASALIS. And?

SPEER. I said: 'You've got it upside down'.

Behind SPEER, *Germania is beginning to materialise.*

CASALIS. Yes of course. It is possible to read too much into these things. Please do go on.

SPEER. And then one day in 1936 I was told there was another job for me. 'The greatest and the best of all'. Well, even he had got to be impressed with *this*.

CASALIS (*surprised*). uh – Hitler?

SPEER (*suddenly aware of his slippage*). My father.

1.5   General Inspectorate, Berlin, 1938

*Suddenly through the darkness we see a vision of the new
Berlin at night. In fact, it is the model of Speer's design for the
city Hitler would call Germania, 100 metres long, erected in
the basement of the General Inspectorate of Buildings, Speer's
office in Berlin. We understand this when what initially
appears to be a giant appears behind the huge, domed hall at
the end of the main north-south axis. It is Speer's 75-year-old*
FATHER. *He has a scrap of paper he tries to look at in the
gloom. He looks at the model. Then he calls:*

FATHER. I am looking . . . I understand this is . . . I am
    looking for the headquarters of the General Inspectorate . . .

Lights come on, illuminating the model. Enter WOLTERS
followed by ANNEMARIE.

WOLTERS. Herr Speer, how good to see you.

ANNEMARIE. We didn't know that you'd arrived.

ANNEMARIE *nods to* WOLTERS *to go off and find*
SPEER. WOLTERS *goes.*

FATHER. I lost . . . I must have come round the wrong way.
    There was a garden and a little door . . .

ANNEMARIE. My name is Annemarie Wittenberg. I am your
    son's secretary.

FATHER. He has a secretary?

ANNEMARIE. Oh, he has a staff of 85!

She sees SPEER *coming in and goes to him.*

SPEER. Sir, you're here.

ANNEMARIE (*whispers*). He came in through the
    Chancellory entrance.

SPEER *is going to his* FATHER. *They shake hands.*

FATHER. Albert.

SPEER. You are welcome, sir.

Pause. SPEER *waits for his* FATHER *to acknowledge the model.*

FATHER. You're not in party uniform.

SPEER. No, I wear civilian clothes.

Pause.

FATHER (*to* ANNEMARIE). He was always slovenly in dress, as a young man.

SPEER. Sir, you will remember Rudi Wolters.

FATHER *looks to the only person* WOLTERS *can be.*

FATHER. Yes. I think I do.

WOLTERS. How are you sir?

FATHER. I am so-so.

SPEER *is growing desperate.*

SPEER. How is my mother?

FATHER. She is in good spirits. As are both your brothers.

Slight pause.

How is your family?

ANNEMARIE *can't bear it any more.*

ANNEMARIE. Herr Speer, this is the model for the new Berlin.

FATHER. Yes so I see.

A telephone rings offstage.

ANNEMARIE. Herr Wolters, I'm sure Herr Speer would welcome a short interpretation.

ANNEMARIE *goes out to answer the telephone. The* FATHER *looks at the model as* WOLTERS *starts the usual pitch.*

WOLTERS. Well, sir. The overall principle is the intersection of four thoroughfares of equal width, themselves linked \ at their extremities with the autobahn –

FATHER. So where's the south station?

Re-enter ANNEMARIE *in some concern.*

SPEER. Well, sir, in fact, the reordering of rail is Herr Wolters prime responsibility/. I'm sure –

FATHER. And the Tiergarten?

SPEER. But the major feature is the North-South axis flanked by state and representative buildings, 120 metres wide and five kilometres long running from –

FATHER. Ah. the figures. Always Albert and his figures. You know he wanted to do mathematics as a life career?

SPEER. Yes, sir. And it was you who persuaded me to change my mind.

ANNEMARIE (*whispers*). The Chief is on his way.

SPEER (*whispers*). He's *what*?

FATHER. Rather than end up at a dead-end university, cramming little mediocrities to scrape through their exams.

SPEER. Well, I think we can agree that between us we took the right decision. But now, sir, I am told that we have guests . . .

FATHER. What at this hour?

The door at the back opens and Colonel VON BELOW *admits* HITLER *with* FRAU VON BELOW, *20*, FRAU ANNI BRANDT, *33, and* EVA BRAUN, *26.*

HITLER. Come, come, this is much better.

SPEER. Yes, at this hour.

EVA BRAUN (*seeing the model*). Oh, look!

FRAU VON BELOW (*to* VON BELOW). What's this?

HITLER (*barring the model*). Stop. Now.

VON BELOW. The Führer \ will outline –

HITLER. – will explain. I have always said: a new nation needs new buildings, most especially in its capital. Ladies and gentlemen, Germania.

A 'reveal' gesture.

EVA BRAUN. Well, look at that.

FRAU VON BELOW. Aha.

HITLER. And, see – here is its creator.

FRAU BRANDT. Good evening, Herr Speer.

SPEER (*trying to introduce his* FATHER). My Führer,/ may I introduce –

HITLER. We have all been looking at some movie. It is stupid. I ring Goebbels, 'what is this stupid film? In the bin with it, in the bin!' Now shall you explain it or shall I?

SPEER. My Führer, \ I would like you –

HITLER (*prompting*). The principle . . .

SPEER (*giving up*). The principle is the meeting of four equal thoroughfares, linked \ at their extremities –

HITLER. Yes, yes, yes. But *this*.

SPEER. Well, starting with the east-west axis, running \ along what is now –

HITLER. No. No. Starting with the North-South axis, here, Frau von Below, five kilometres long, 120 metres wide, do you know what that is wider than?

FRAU VON BELOW. No, I don't my Führer.

HITLER. The Champs Elysée! Come, Frau Brandt, look here . . .

FRAU BRANDT. And those presumably are trees?

HITLER. But unlike Paris, not flanked with plutocratic utilitarian buildings, not by banks, but by monumental architecture, theatres, opera houses . . . Come, Fräulein Braun, Frau von Below, come, look here.

EVA BRAUN. Um, where?

HITLER *is making* FRAU BRANDT, FRAU VON BELOW *and* EVA BRAUN *look through the arch up the boulevard to the domed palace.*

HITLER. No, bend, through there . . .

FRAU BRANDT. Oh, yes, do you see, Fräulein Braun?

HITLER. The view through Speer's triumphal arch.

SPEER. *Your* triumphal arch, my Führer.

EVA BRAUN. Yes, I can see, my Führer.

FRAU VON BELOW. Quite magnificent.

HITLER. Itself 72 metres taller than the Arc de Triomphe, bearing the names of the 1.8 million German war dead, leading to . . .

He runs up the North-South axis.

. . . the largest building in the world. Speer, Speer, tell us the dimensions.

SPEER. Well, it is designed to be 290 metres high.

HITLER. And seating . . .

SPEER. My Führer, you always have these figures at your fingertips.

HITLER. One hundred and eighty thousand people!

FRAU VON BELOW. Goodness.

EVA BRAUN (*whispers to* ANNEMARIE). What are those?

ANNEMARIE. They're fountains, Fräulein.

FRAU BRANDT. The trees are very beautiful.

HITLER. While here is my new Chancellory, which Speer has promised me will be ready on the 10th of January 1939.

SPEER. As it will be.

HITLER. And do you know *how* Herr Speer will make this ready for the 10th of January next year?

EVA BRAUN. No, my Führer.

HITLER. By placing orders first for those items which take longest to produce. Which are?

FRAU VON BELOW. I've really no idea.

HITLER. The carpets! Can you believe that? It's the carpets. With a logistic sense like that, this man should head the General Staff!

SPEER. My Führer, I am quite content with my present duties.

HITLER. But you must introduce me to your father.

ALL *look at* SPEER*'s* FATHER.

FRAU BRANDT. Ah.

HITLER. Who taught you I have no doubt everything you know.

HITLER *goes to the* FATHER, *gives a kind of bow. Nervously, the* FATHER *puts his hand out.* HITLER *shakes it, but holds on, cupping the* FATHER*'s elbow and turning the gesture into a kind of embrace.*

May I introduce Frau Brandt, who is married to my doctor. Fräulein Braun, who is visiting from Munich. My military adjutant, Colonel von Below and Frau von Below. Ladies and gentlemen, the father of my architect!

He turns back to focus on SPEER'S FATHER, *who remains struck dumb.*

They say I am obsessed with height and width and depth. But it is all your son. I say – 200 metres. He says – why not three?

He looks into SPEER'S FATHER*'s eyes.*

Now. You have the Führer. And his architect. And his plan to build a capital that will outshine even Paris, the greatest capital existing in the world. Is there anything you want to ask?

Pause.

FATHER. I would . . . I . . . as you raise the matter of the future, I would be interested to know . . . where the people, in the houses you are going to demolish . . . where they will go.

HITLER *suddenly snaps round to* SPEER.

HITLER. Well? That's a question!

SPEER (*unusually thrown*). Um . . .

During this SCHAUB *enters and comes forward.*

WOLTERS (*to the rescue*). There is of course a comprehensive plan for the rehousing of those persons who are dispossessed. Garden suburbs will be built in which these people can be housed. Overall, the housing plan for the new Berlin \ will accommodate –

SPEER (*back on track*). The plan overall is to house eight million people.

HITLER (*to the* FATHER). There. You have the answer.

SCHAUB. My Führer. They have found another film.

HITLER. Well, let's hope it's better than the last.

The company, a little relieved, is moving to go. Again suddenly, HITLER *returns to* SPEER'S FATHER.

My esteemed Herr Speer. Your son is a philosopher. He builds with distant posterity in mind. He makes drawings of how the ruins of his buildings might appear when overgrown, abandoned, in a thousand years from now. Like the Pyramids or Agrigento or the Parthenon. What is left of a great age but its monuments? Your son has understood that. He is creating them.

SPEER'S FATHER *is looking down, a kind of strange bow.*

I too was a son who told his father that he yearned to be an artist. There the similarity ends. He told me that this was unthinkable. No! Never! What a thought!

SPEER'S FATHER *is shaking.*

Well, I have always said, my mission is to realise the hitherto unthinkable.

HITLER *puts out his hand to* SPEER'S FATHER, *who does not respond. Quickly, turning to go.*

What a father! What a son!

HITLER *walks to* SPEER, *cups his arm, and walks quickly out.*

FRAU BRANDT. Goodnight, Herr Speer. I hope . . . your father . . .

FRAU BRANDT, EVA BRAUN, VON BELOW, SCHAUB *follow* HITLER *out.* SPEER *goes to his* FATHER, *tries to take his arm, but his* FATHER *pulls his arm away.*

ANNEMARIE. Perhaps, Herr Speer . . . it's very late.

SPEER (*to* ANNEMARIE). Go and call the car.

ANNEMARIE *goes out.*

SPEER (*to his* FATHER). He always likes to better me on figures.

FATHER. Hm.

SPEER. But once, I had to tell him that he was in error. We were discussing plans for the development of the Olympic Stadium. I pointed out that the athletic field did not conform to the dimensions laid down by the Federation. He replied that in 1940 the games will be in Tokyo. But after that, for all time to come, they will be here. And it will be us who will decide the necessary dimensions.

Re-enter ANNEMARIE.

ANNEMARIE. The car is here.

Slight pause.

SPEER. So, sir. What do you think?

FATHER *looks at* SPEER.

FATHER. I think – you've all gone insane.

He goes quickly out. ANNEMARIE *looks back wide-eyed and then follows.* SPEER *to* WOLTERS.

WOLTERS. He's wrong.

SPEER. I showed Tessenow the designs for Nuremberg. He said: 'They're big, that's all'.

WOLTERS. They are both wrong. How could they not be?

Slight pause.

You have not begun, Herr General Inspector.

SPEER *smiles, and clasps his friend.*

SPEER. 'To have young men about me, for whom the word impossible . . . '

WOLTERS *turns to go.*

Will you do the lights?

WOLTERS. Of course.

WOLTERS *turns down the lights to a night effect and goes.*
SPEER *looks at the model in the 'moonlight'. Suddenly the door at the back opens.* HITLER *re-enters.*

HITLER. Well, the second film was rubbish too. What did he think?

SPEER. It is hard for people of his age.

HITLER. Of course. And you are pulled two ways. You love your father, as your father. But your greater love is for your Fatherland. You must not feel guilty, it is rightly so.

Pause. HITLER *looks at the model, bathed in the moonlight.*

I can tell so few. My mission is to unify a single people in a single state. We are going to create a vast new Empire, combining all Germanic peoples, from Norway down to northern Italy. And your buildings, here, will crown that great achievement. Do you understand now why they must be huge? The capital of the Germanic Reich?

He goes and puts his hand on the top of the dome.

There are two possibilities. To win through, or to fail.
If I win, I will be the greatest man since Charlemagne. If I lose – well, all this might just as well be dust. Goodnight.

SPEER. Heil, my Führer.

HITLER. Heil Speer.

HITLER *goes out.*

1.6.1   Spandau, 1947–50

Enter CASALIS *to* SPEER.

CASALIS. So what do you suppose he meant?

SPEER. Hitler?

CASALIS. Your father.

SPEER. He meant that he didn't understand, like so many of his generation.

CASALIS. I meant, what did your father mean by saying nothing?

SPEER *smiles and shrugs, as if this is all a little metaphysical.*

You said, when Hitler spoke to him, he bowed and trembled and said nothing. And when afterwards you tried to take his arm he pulled away.

SPEER. Yes?

CASALIS. I wondered if he sensed something that you didn't sense, yourself, till later.

SPEER. What, a 'sense of evil'?

CASALIS *acknowledges.*

Herr Pastor, this was 1938.

CASALIS. So Hitler was not evil at that stage?

SPEER. Look. Of course, we knew that Hitler sought world domination. What my father didn't understand, and you don't understand, is that at the time we asked for nothing better. Eighty million Germans didn't follow Hitler because he was going to murder people in lime ditches and gas chambers. They didn't follow him because they knew that he was evil, but because they thought he was extremely good.

SPEER *puts on his leather overcoat and cap.*

And I'm afraid, most strongly in June 1940, at the fall of France. When in defiance of the whiners and the moaners, he had the world before him. And he laid it at my feet.

1.6.2   Paris, June 1940

The German anthem. HITLER *and his* ENTOURAGE *stride forward in a line, joined by* SPEER. CASALIS *watches.*

HITLER. I tell you. It was always my dream, to be permitted to see Paris. Haussman's Boulevards. Les Invalides. I could have walked around Charles Garnier's opera in blindfolds.

In three months, London will be rubble. And when you have finished, even Paris will be but a shadow.

SPEER *turns back to* CASALIS.

SPEER. It was his dream. Though of course if you want to visit Paris it isn't strictly necessary to overthrow the government of France.

And then and there he ordered me to draw up a decree for the commencement of the reconstruction of Berlin. How could I not be his, then, body and soul?

HITLER *looks at* SPEER *in triumph, turns and goes.*

CASALIS. So you had your Mephistophilis.

SPEER. And he had his Faust.

And then one evening in his mountaintop retreat, when we had thought he'd long since gone to bed, he told me how he planned to crown his Paris triumph with an even greater victory.

1.6.3   Berghof, Obersaltzberg, July 1941

Two YOUNG ADJUTANTS, *two* SECRETARIES –
FRÄULEIN JOHANNA WOLF *and* FRÄULEIN CHRISTA
SCHRÖDER *run in – followed by* FRAU BRANDT *and*
MARGRET. *The* FIRST ADJUTANT *holds a large peaked
cap. There is a piano in the room.*

FRAU BRANDT. No you *mustn't*.

FIRST ADJUTANT. I'm shaking! It's heavy in my hands!

MARGRET. What's going on?

FRAU BRANDT. Very schoolboyish behaviour.

FRÄULEIN SCHRÖDER. Oh for God's sake give it here.

She takes the cap.

There are, after all, but two possibilities.

SECOND ADJUTANT. One being that no one puts his hat on.

FRÄULEIN SCHRÖDER. And the other is that someone does.

FRAU BRANDT. Well, on your own heads be it.

FRÄULEIN SCHRÖDER *puts the cap on. It's far too big.
The others laugh and applaud.*

FRÄULEIN SCHRÖDER. Tara tara. Who's next?

FIRST ADJUTANT. In such times one cannot use Salvation
Army methods.

He puts the cap on. It's far too big.

FRÄULEIN SCHRÖDER. Extreme times call for extreme
measures!

The FIRST ADJUTANT *puts the cap on. It's far too big.
He looks round for the next person to try it.*

FIRST ADJUTANT. And now, Frau Brandt . . .

FRAU BRANDT. Oh no.

FRÄULEIN WOLF. Herr Speer?

SPEER *diffident.*

SPEER. Um . . . I . . .

MARGRET. Albert.

FRÄULEIN WOLF (*winningly*). Herr Speer.

Pause. SPEER *takes the cap.*

SPEER. Well, I have always said, my mission is to bring the unthinkable about.

He puts the cap on. It fits. Surprised applause. EVA BRAUN *has entered.*

EVA BRAUN. Dear Herr Speer, what are you doing?

She gestures offstage just in time for SPEER *to rip the cap from his head and put it behind his back, before* HITLER *and* VON BELOW *enter, the latter carrying sheet music.*

HITLER. Ladies and gentlemen, my profound apologies.

FRAU BRANDT. Well, it's past bedtime . . .

Suddenly HITLER *goes to* MARGRET, *kisses her hand.*

HITLER. My own Frau Speer. Gracious ladies. Gentlemen.

Everyone takes this as a dismissal.

MARGRET. Goodnight, my Führer.

She goes out, the OTHERS *follow, murmuring 'Goodnight' and 'Goodnight, my Führer'.* HITLER *a slight gesture to* SPEER *to stay.*

HITLER. Perhaps you too, my little applecake. Colonel, please.

EVA BRAUN *shrugs. She goes to* SPEER.

SPEER. Goodnight, Fräulein Braun.

With a slight gesture to SPEER.

EVA BRAUN. Goodnight, oh my dear Herr Speer. And goodnight my Führer.

She turns back and smiles at HITLER, *taking the cap from* SPEER *with her back hand. She goes.*

VON BELOW *sits at the piano and plays a fanfare from Liszt's Les Preludes.*

SPEER. It's Liszt?

HITLER. Yes. It's from the Preludes. So what d'you think of it?

SPEER. I suppose, my Führer, that depends on what it's for.

HITLER. This will be 'for' the decisive confrontation of our epoch. Of course I am told I must 'negotiate' with our enemies. That traitor Hess flies off to Scotland to sue for peace with that alcoholic gangster Churchill. But I say that we are now engaged in the final battle between Western civilisation and the international Jew-Bolshevik conspiracy. Our aim must be nothing less than the complete destruction of that criminal conspiracy, with implacable and iron zeal. Naturally I am told this is unthinkable. But I say, one good strong German kick, and the whole rotten edifice falls in.

SPEER. Russia.

HITLER. Yes.

He looks at SPEER. *It's the stare game. Without taking his eye off* SPEER.

HITLER. The victory fanfare. You will hear it frequently.

He holds the stare.

And for those who make the final sacrifice, your Germania will stand as their memorial for ever; the names of our heroic fallen carved on every stone.

Finally, HITLER *breaks the stare, then goes to* SPEER *and cups his elbow.*

And you will have all the granite and the marble that you need.

The fanfare continues orchestrally. Exit HITLER *and* VON BELOW. SPEER *turns to* CASALIS. *Behind him, a dark void from which snow billows.*

SPEER. But it was clear within months of the actual invasion of the Soviet Union that there were much more immediate construction needs.

1.7.1   Ukraine, February 1942

Outside, at night, in the winter snow. SPEER *in a heavy overcoat. Enter* WOLTERS, *also heavily overcoated. Enter a young railway engineer, Theodor* GANZENMÜLLER, *with a mess-tin of caviare and spoons.*

GANZENMÜLLER. Ah, Herr Wolters, please try this.

WOLTERS. What is it?

GANZENMÜLLER. It's the real stuff.

WOLTERS. Herr Ganzenmüller, this is General Inspector Speer.

GANZENMÜLLER. Welcome to the Ukraine, sir. Please try some caviare.

WOLTERS. Herr Ganzenmüller is performing miracles with what we must call for want of any better term the Ukraine railway system.

SPEER. Well, I'm all for miracles.

He takes caviare.

That's good.

Enter a group of SPEER CONSTRUCTION WORKERS *and* SOLDIERS, *led by a* MAJOR, MUSICIANS *and two* TUFTIES – *young Ukrainian women* – *with trays of glasses and vodka.*

MAJOR. Now after so many cheerful days with the Speer Construction Squad can this be Herr Speer himself? Tufty One, vodka for Herr Speer!

SPEER. Tufty?

WOLTERS. Ukrainian girls.

MAJOR. You will find this a change from building palaces and opera houses.

SPEER takes vodka from one TUFTY, *as the other hands vodka out to the rest.*

SPEER. It is a change which I enthusiastically proposed, Herr Major. Over half my workforce is assisting with reconstruction work in Russia.

MAJOR. A toast! In acknowledgement of Herr General Inspector's visit from Berlin! To our matchless constructional facilities! To our Repair Sheds!

FIRST SPEER SQUAD. Water tanks.

MAJOR. To our insulated water tanks!

SECOND SPEER SQUAD. Lumber!

THIRD SPEER SQUAD. Tracking!

FOURTH SPEER SQUAD. Nails!

All drink. Recovering from the hit:

SPEER. Well, in that case, all these things will be provided instantly. Herr Wolters, see to it at once.

Cheers, on the edge of mockery, but ambiguous enough for the MAJOR *to move on.*

MAJOR. Then – music!

Sad music is played. The MEN *move upstage.*

SPEER (*to* GANZENMÜLLER). So the problem is supplies.

GANZENMÜLLER. Supplies of the right thing at the right time. Guns, no ammo. Tanks, no fuel. Troops, no trains.

SPEER. You mean it's not production, it's logistics.

GANZENMÜLLER. Of course I needn't tell you this. The man who worked out that the first thing that you have to order for a building is the carpeting.

SPEER (*smiles*). Yes.

GANZENMÜLLER. Apparently, the war economy was two
days from collapse through a shortage of ball-bearings.

He does a gesture – a machine turning.

Work it out.

SPEER. Oh, I don't need to.

GANZENMÜLLER *is fearful he may have gone too far.*

GANZENMÜLLER. But then again, we both know the order:
'Everyone need only know what is going on in his domain'.

The MAJOR *approaches.*

SPEER. And may I ask, is all this typical? This gloomy music?

Pause.

GANZENMÜLLER. It is typical of men so far from home.

SPEER. In circumstances such as these.

MAJOR. And up against what they are up against.

WOLTERS. The elements?

MAJOR. The enemy.

SPEER *looks surprised.*

Oh yes, Herr Speer. First thing you learn about the Ivan,
don't underestimate his natural resourcefulness. Give
him an axe, in a few hours time he'll have knocked up
anything. A sledge, an igloo . . . And the way they use that
damned T-34.

WOLTERS. The tank.

MAJOR. The tank . . . the pillbox, the bivouak, the bulldozer . . .
And Army Group Centre enters Russia with 2,000 different
types of vehicle.

GANZENMÜLLER. And a million spare parts.

MAJOR. And all they're issued with is fuel and ammo. So if
they need spare parts, they rip 'em from the wrecks. Oh,
yes, despite the propaganda, we have an enemy.

SPEER. The propaganda?

MAJOR. Surely you've heard the shit. 'One good strong kick, and the whole rotten edifice falls in'.

A moment of stand off, between SPEER *and the* MAJOR.

And you know they say you have to kill each Ivan twice. And no one who draws blood here leaves the place alive.

SPEER. And I'm sure you discourage such defeatist talk, Herr Major. Concentrating solely on ensuring that these brave young men are properly supplied. As will I.

MAJOR. But of course, Herr General Inspector.

The MAJOR *goes out.*

GANZENMÜLLER. And now you will forgive me. Tomorrow I have to open up a railway line as far as Sinelnikovo. With the assistance of the Speer Construction Squad, and a goodly slice of the surrounding peasantry.

SPEER. And they are collaborative?

GANZENMÜLLER. Collaborative and numerous. Goodnight, Herr Speer.

He goes out.

WOLTERS. Apparently, the chaps say that the Jewish details are the best. They work double shifts, even voluntarily. Of course, they know \ that if they don't –

SPEER. That Ganzenmüller is presumably the best man we have.

WOLTERS. A man for whom the word impossible does not exist?

SPEER. Exactly and precisely so.

They stand listening to the music for a moment.

I have a brother, out here, somewhere, Rudi.

The scene disperses.

SPEER. And so on the evening of the 7th February I arrived at Hitler's eastern field HQ, hoping to report to the Minister of Armaments, Dr Todt, who had built the autobahns and to

whom I was, in a sense at least, now working. But when
I arrived I was informed that Dr Todt had been with Hitler
for some time. And later that he was in the operations room.

1.8   Operations Room of Rastenberg barracks, 7 February 1942

*Dominated by a huge table map of Europe, the room bears
evidence of a long day – papers, half eaten pastries, trays of
coffee long since gone cold. At the back are two young* STAFF
OFFICERS *taking information from telephones; occasionally
they move forward to move a flag on the map. At the moment,
the room is empty apart from* TODT *who stands looking at the
map, a brandy glass in his hand. Enter* SPEER *with a bottle of
champagne and two glasses.*

TODT. Champagne?

SPEER. Champagne.

> SPEER *pours* TODT *a glass of champagne and hands it
> over, as:*

TODT. Maybe we should have stuck to France.

SPEER. Ah, but I hear the Georgian wines are marvellous.

TODT. Oh, well, then. Let's plough on.

> SPEER *laughs, as a* STAFF OFFICER *moves forward with
> an intelligence report.*

SPEER. How is the Chief?

STAFF OFFICER. Heil Hitler, Herr Reichsminister.

TODT. 'Hitler.

> TODT *doesn't want to answer* SPEER's *question with
> someone listening. The* STAFF OFFICER *moves a flag on
> the map, as*:

TODT. So how long are you here for?

SPEER. I should leave tomorrow. On that ghastly train.

The STAFF OFFICER *withdraws.*

TODT. Speer, have you actually read *Mein Kampf*?

SPEER. Well, not exactly. In fact, I told the Chief. He said not to bother, it had been overtaken by events.

TODT. Well, yes, in some respects. However.

He takes out a notebook and reads from it.

'The task of diplomacy is to ensure that a nation does not heroically perish, but that measures are taken to preserve it'.

Pause.

SPEER. So what's the relevance of that?

TODT. It is relevant to what I've spent the last two hours trying to explain to him.

SPEER. Which is?

TODT. That if we haven't beaten Russia by Christmas then we've lost the war.

SPEER *has to ask the question:*

SPEER. So, why?

TODT. American technology, and Russian space. I mean, just look at it.

SPEER. Well, yes \ but on the other –

TODT. Oh, and your housekeeper.

SPEER. My housekeeper?

TODT. You have one?

SPEER. Yes.

TODT. And your maid. And maybe a governess?

SPEER. I've got five children.

TODT. We are in the third year of what is now a world war. And we employ the same number of domestic servants as we did in 1939. And when you raise the possibility of mobilising women workers, *like* the Russians, *like* the British, you are told about the moral threat to German womanhood. Oh, and look.

There's a tray of coffee things. He picks up a paper-wrapped sugar cube from the sugar bowl.

We're still wrapping sugar-cubes in pretty paper.

SPEER. I understand you were two days away from running out of ball-bearings.

TODT. No, worse. We were nearly out of screws.

SPEER. Who'd have your job?

TODT. Oh, Speer.

The other STAFF OFFICER *comes forward, to move a flag.* SPEER *and* TODT *notice that he moves the flag that his colleague moved forward back.* TODT *is a little drunk.*

Hey. You don't want that shitty train. I'm flying to Berlin at daybreak. Want a ride?

The STAFF OFFICER *withdraws.* SPEER, *trying something out:*

SPEER. Of course . . . in fact, there's millions. Men *and* women. In the east. Collaborative and numerous.

TODT. Aha. The 'Slav subhumans'.

SPEER. Yes. But what I meant \ was that they might –

TODT. I'm sorry. You're a young man. You think solutions. I just – brood.

SPEER *smiles, as if to say 'don't worry'.*

I'll see you on the plane.

TODT *goes.* SCHAUB *enters. During the following, the young* STAFF OFFICERS *go too.*

SCHAUB. Herr General Inspector. You're still up.

SPEER. Yes. Though I think I'm going to bed.

SCHAUB. He wants to see you.

SPEER (*looks at his watch*). Oh, can't you tell him . . .

SCHAUB. He is on his way.

Enter HITLER. SCHAUB *salutes.*

'Hitler!

HITLER *acknowledges.* SCHAUB *goes out.* HITLER *is still ruffled from his conversation with* TODT, *but suppressing it.*

HITLER. My dear Speer. How are you?

SPEER. My Führer. Very well. Perhaps a little tired.

HITLER. How are Frau Speer and your family?

SPEER. I fear I haven't seen them in a while.

HITLER. You have been in the Ukraine. Now don't remind me. Albert, Hilde . . . Fritz, Margaret . . . Ernst.

SPEER. Arnold. Who is nearly two. Ernst is my brother.

HITLER (*that explains it*). Ah.

SPEER. Who is a little more than two.

HITLER. And presumably . . .

SPEER. Serves in the sixth at Krasnograd.

HITLER. Ah. There are bold and heroic deeds in prospect for the Sixth. So, Arnold nearly two.

SPEER (*smiling*). In fact, I'm going home tomorrow.

HITLER. Not by train I trust. I will have von Below get you on a flight.

SPEER. Thank you, my Führer. But I have arranged a lift with the minister of armaments first thing.

HITLER. Oh, have you?

Slight pause.

SPEER. I saw him earlier.

HITLER. Yes, so did I.

Slight pause.

SPEER. He seemed . . .

HITLER. Speer, we live in times when only optimists can achieve anything. The trouble with Herr Todt is that he is fundamentally and unshakably a pessimist. Whose pessimism extends beyond his own domain, to matters which do not concern him.

SPEER. I think he is worried about the labour problem.

HITLER. I know. But I will *not* drive German women from their homes.

SPEER *takes the sugar cube from his pocket.*

SPEER. I think he feels that under total war \ there are some things –

HITLER *picks up a sugar cube and eats it.*

HITLER. And I will not deny them some at least of the things that make life civilised and elegant.

SPEER *puts the sugar cube back in his pocket.*

SPEER. When of course . . . we have twenty million potential men and women workers under our control.

HITLER. Well exactly. Twenty million Slav subhumans. Leaderless, supine, with no defence against the Jew-Communist embrace. I tell you, Speer, now is not the time to use Salvation Army methods! Set them all to work!

SPEER. Well, of course it is not precisely my area of responsibility –

HITLER. No. You are not Dr Todt.

HITLER *goes to* SPEER *and pats his shoulder.*

Your charming wife. Your lovely family. From Albert down to Arnold nearly two. Yet your absolute priority? The greater German good.

Slight pause.

I am adamant about the women. But it may be . . . that we should ensure that production for the civilian market . . . is in proportion to the national need.

SPEER. Well, I'm sure \ that would be –

HITLER. What is the time?

SPEER. I fear \ it's very late –

HITLER (*looks at* SPEER*'s watch*). You're going to fly in three hours' time?

SPEER. Well, I . . .

HITLER. It's up to you.

Pause.

Sometimes, I regret what history requires of me. One cannot be the Führer all one's life. This war is robbing me of my best years. Sometimes I think, I should hang up my field grey jacket and go home to Linz, my birthplace on the Danube, where my remains will lie . . . But I have burnt my bridges. So have you.

Slight pause.

You know, it may well be . . . that I will need to speak with you tomorrow.

He looks at SPEER.

Shall I have von Below call the pilot?

SPEER. No, I'll do it.

HITLER. Well.

Slight pause.

You're right. Twenty million foreign workers. Teach them to read roadsigns. Tell them the capital of Germany's Germania. And work them all like dogs to death. Goodnight.

SPEER. Heil my Führer!

HITLER. And Heil Speer.

HITLER *goes. Darkness. We hear the sound of an aeroplane taking off and then immediately spiralling down to crash.*

1.9.1   Courtyard of the Ministry of Armaments,
9 February 1942. Morning

It's snowing. A microphone has been set up in the courtyard.
ANNEMARIE *and* WOLTERS *enter.* OFFICIALS *from the*
Ministry of Armaments have gathered, including the senior
STATE SECRETARY *and his young male administrative*
ASSISTANT. *As* SPEER *enters to the microphone, he takes*
off his overcoat. He is in uniform, with a swastika armband.
He hands his coat to ANNEMARIE.

ANNEMARIE. But, Herr Speer . . .

SPEER. It's all right, Wittenberg.

> ANNEMARIE *glances questioningly at* WOLTERS, *who*
> *shrugs, as* SPEER *begins to speak.*

SPEER. Party Comrades! Esteemed employees of the Ministry
of Armaments! It is my sad duty to report that at the zenith
of his labours, your leader Reichsminister Professor Todt
was taken from you yesterday in a plane crash in East Prussia.

Shock.

The Führer has placed me in charge of all Dr Todt's roles
and functions.

People look at each other.

I have proposed – and the Führer has agreed – to free our
war production industries from the shackles of duplication
and bureaucracy. I have recommended – and the Führer has
enthusiastically approved – the severest penalties for the use
of materials, machinery or manpower for unauthorised or
private purposes. With the Führer's keen endorsement, I
have ordered the full mobilisation of up to twenty million
workers from the conquered territories.

A little applause; alarm from the STATE SECRETARY.

I have nothing else to say. We have a war to win and we
shall win it. Sieg Heil!

SPEER *leaves the microphone.*

STATE SECRETARY. Well, congratulations, Herr
Reichsminister.

The REST *dispersing. We see an army private, on the edge
of the crowd, waiting. It is Speer's brother* ERNST.

SPEER. Thank you, State Secretary. Rudi, have Wittenberg call
up that railway engineer we met in the Ukraine.

STATE SECRETARY. However, I must respectfully enquire \
about the matter of –

WOLTERS. You mean, the one for whom the word
'impossible' . . . ?

SPEER. Precisely so.

STATE SECRETARY. . . . as to what specifically is meant by
'freeing war production from duplication and bureaucracy'. \
As of course –

SPEER. I think he is about to be promoted. Yes, State Secretary?

STATE SECRETARY. And . . . exactly what is meant by it.

SPEER. Well, certainly, I am eager to discuss all aspects of the
new production policy. Do I have an office?

STATE SECRETARY. Yes of course.

ANNEMARIE. Herr Speer, there is something I must ask you.

SPEER. I will be with you in a moment.

WOLTERS *and the* STATE SECRETARY *go.*

SPEER. Of course, I didn't realise at first. I thought he meant
for me \ to take over Todt's construction work –

ANNEMARIE. Herr Speer, do you intend for me to remain
your secretary in your new post?

SPEER. Of course.

ANNEMARIE. Because if so I would like a day or two to
think about it.

ERNST. Albert.

SPEER. What?

He turns to see ERNST.

ANNEMARIE. And as I have already booked a holiday . . .

SPEER. Why – Ernst.

ANNEMARIE. Perhaps you wouldn't mind . . .

SPEER. Please, Wittenberg . . . a moment.

ANNEMARIE *thrown by the sight of* SPEER*'s brother.*

ANNEMARIE. Yes of course.

SPEER. Ernst, why are you here?

ANNEMARIE. But it is Frau Kempf, Herr Speer. As you may recall, you commissioned me to buy a present for my wedding.

She goes out, leaving SPEER *and* ERNST *alone.*

ERNST. Here in Berlin? On leave. Here at your ministry? Our mother telephoned me with your news. She said that I should come at once so you could get me out.

Enter the STATE SECRETARY'S ASSISTANT.

ASSISTANT. Reichsminister, I have to tell you that the State Secretary is waiting.

SPEER. I will be with him in a moment. What d'you mean?

The ASSISTANT *goes out.*

ERNST. I mean that you get me transferred to the west.

SPEER. Oh Ernst you know I can't do that.

ERNST. Whyever not? You're the Minister of Armaments.

SPEER. But I have been appointed quite specifically to stamp out \ special favours –

ERNST. Our mother said you would. She said you'd do this for her sake.

Enter WOLTERS.

WOLTERS. Albert, the natives are \ getting restless –

SPEER. One *moment*. Ernst, I'll do my best. I shouldn't but I will.

ERNST. To do what?

SPEER. To get you transferred to the west. Now, Rudi . . .

ERNST. Oh, Albert. When?

SPEER. Well, obviously, at the end of this campaign.

ERNST (*desperate*). I'm sorry . . . ?

SPEER. Rudi, please tell them that I'm on \ my way . . .

ERNST. Well, then, that's that. We are preparing the advance towards the Volga.

The STATE SECRETARY *is coming out into the courtyard.*

STATE SECRETARY. Now, I am so sorry, Herr Reichs-minister –

ERNST. So, till we meet again, Herr Professor Speer.

He salutes.

SPEER. Ernst, please, a moment –

STATE SECRETARY. But if you are to alter Ministry practices and protocols to the extent that you imply, then I will need to know on what authority \ these proposals have been made and who will be deemed responsible –

ERNST. I'm sorry. I will miss my train.

SPEER. Ernst, stay. State Secretary, it is not me implying any-thing. It is implementing what the Führer has commanded. That is 'my authority'.

ERNST. Heil Hitler!

He clicks his heels, salutes, turns, and goes quickly out, SPEER *turns back to him.*

SPEER. Ernst . . . What?

Turning back.

Do you see?

Outflanked, the STATE SECRETARY *senses that he must leave and be followed.*

STATE SECRETARY. I await you in your office, Herr Reichsminister.

He goes out.

WOLTERS. Your brother?

SPEER. Yes. He's a private with the sixth.

WOLTERS. I know, you told me. So what really happened in East Prussia?

SPEER (*still looking after* ERNST). I thought he meant I was to take on Todt's construction work. I didn't know he wanted me to be the Minister of Armaments.

WOLTERS. I meant, what happened to Herr Todt?

SPEER *turns back to his old friend.*

SPEER. Apparently, there was diminished visibility . . . It's thought the pilot couldn't make out the horizon.

WOLTERS. Ah.

SPEER. But of course . . . this matter isn't our domain.

1.9.2   Berlin, November 1942

SPEER *turns to* CASALIS.

SPEER. So what was I to do? I didn't even shake his hand. And then as the weeks went by there was my father.

SPEER'S FATHER *appears.*

FATHER. He's in an advanced observation unit. He is ill. He is your brother. Surely you, you of all people, can get him out.

SPEER. And as the months, my mother.

FATHER *disappears,* ANNEMARIE *appears.*

ANNEMARIE. She rang again today. Five times. She said you can't do this to him.

ANNEMARIE *disappears.*

SPEER. I had been given what was probably the second most important job in Germany, at a time of national peril. And I was supposed to put my family before my country?

CASALIS. Your country?

SPEER. Yes of course.

CASALIS. Or your career.

SPEER. And my career. Yes. And why not?

CASALIS *says nothing.*

But still . . . when as the battle raged, I was invited to the grand reopening of the Berlin State Opera, sumptuously restored . . .

Enter MARGRET, *pregnant, in an evening gown.* SPEER *joins her in their row of seats at the opera. They speak quietly to each other.*

MARGRET. Albert, what's Sixth Army disease?

SPEER. Jaundice. My mother telephoned.

MARGRET. More than once. Apparently your brother's in a field hospital. With whatever.

SPEER. I know. He wrote to me.

MARGRET. Why can't they fly him out?

SPEER. Because . . . it's not that simple.

MARGRET. Albert, is there something going wrong?

SPEER. No, of course not. Have we ever lost a battle? Have the Russians ever won?

MARGRET. Well, that's all right then. So, what opera are we seeing?

SPEER. The Magic Flute.

MARGRET. Oh good. A fairy tale.

As the overture begins, SPEER *to* CASALIS.

SPEER. And so we sat there in our box in those softly upholstered chairs among this festive audience, and all I could think about was the crowds at the Paris opera during Napoleon's retreat from Moscow.

CASALIS. Did he survive?

SPEER. Towards the end, I asked the people who were flying supplies in to the troops at Stalingrad to try and find him. Apparently, he'd left the so-called field hospital, and dragged himself back to his observation post. And in fact there was one last letter, full of bitterness and rage, against me, his brother.

Pause.

But no they never found him. And my mother told me the wrong brother died.

The opera breaks up and MARGRET *goes.*

1.10.1   Germany 1943

CASALIS. And after Stalingrad? Did you think that maybe Dr Todt was right? And that far from being saviour of Germany, Hitler's actions would destroy your country and its people?

SPEER. Herr Pastor, I have to tell you, that there is an intoxication in the very fact of power. To have the final word, to deal with expenditure in billions . . . But I knew the war would not be won if we continued to refurbish hunting lodges and manufacture ladies' summer outerwear. As I was forced, over the coming months and years, to repeat ad nauseam. Until I finally confronted the assembled Gauleiters of Greater Germany, at the lovingly and lavishly refurbished castle Posen in the Warthegau.

SPEER *is moving to a lectern, lit by candelabra. A little afterthought.*

Where my friend Karl Hanke, now Gauleiter of Lower Silesia, had been primed to put a question.

SPEER *to the lectern. A group of* GAULEITERS *sit in ornate chairs, among them* HANKE.

Yes?

HANKE. Herr Reichsminister. Are you seriously suggesting that those Gauleiters who are not prepared immediately to shut down all consumer goods production in our provinces might face arrest and and even – penal servitude? In concentration camps?

SPEER. Yes, that is exactly what I mean. As the Reichsführer-SS Himmler will underline this afternoon. Next question?

CASALIS. That doesn't answer me.

SPEER. It was the only way to see it, at the time. I was Hitler's Minister of Armaments.

SPEER *leaves the lectern. Enter* HITLER, *furious, to* SPEER, *waving a document.*

HITLER. So what is this?

SPEER *takes the document.*

SPEER. It is a memorandum, on the manganese situation.

HITLER. Which you copied to my chief of staff.

SPEER. My Führer, it's good news. It confirms we have eleven month's supply in Germany.

HITLER. This is intolerable. I have ordered all forces to be concentrated in defence of Nikopol, to the last man and at any cost, precisely to protect its vital manganese. Now I appear a liar and what's worse a fool. You will *not* communicate directly with my chief of staff. You will *not* proceed beyond your own domain.

SPEER (*thrown*). My Führer, naturally, I had no intention \ of giving out a false –

HITLER. Your fault! Your responsibility! Why not admit it, just this once? There are those who say you are the second man in Germany. Do not delude yourself, Herr Speer!

HITLER *storms out.*

CASALIS. But surely the important thing was not your relationship with Hitler but the twenty million foreign workers you had commandeered. Who unlike the Gauleiters were really subject to arrest and servitude in concentration camps.

SPEER. Yes, some of them, of course. This was not the Salvation Army.

CASALIS. And did you know that Hitler ordered physical destruction of the commissars in Russia? That this order was extended to the Jews and gypsies? That his troops were told they would not be held responsible for killing innocent civilans in defiance of the rules of war?

SPEER. No. I did not know of this order.

CASALIS. But surely you had seen a concentration camp?

SPEER. I visited Mauthausen, I think, in March of 1943. But of course, you are a VIP. You see what you are shown. There was a quarry.

CASALIS. Whereas of course thousands of civilians were being sent to camps where the 'special treatment' they received was very different.

SPEER. Of which of course I knew nothing at the time.

CASALIS. But you knew that women, children, old men, were transported . . .

SPEER. Yes of course I did. Every day, as I drove down to the Ministry, I would see crowds of people on the platform of the Nikolassee station. Wearing yellows stars. Presumably, awaiting . . . transportation as you say.

Behind SPEER *we see, through the smoke of the railway station, a* WOMAN *and her elderly* FATHER, *not badly dressed but with meagre luggage and wearing the yellow star.*

CASALIS. And did you not imagine what might lie in store for them?

SPEER. As I said, I had no idea what happened inside
concentration camps.

CASALIS. What no idea? From anything you saw or any place
you visited? What, no idea at all?

Pause. Now, the WOMAN *and her* FATHER *have gone,
and further back in the darkness, through clouds of dust, we
can see a long tunnel, full of still, emaciated creatures, and
hear the insistent sounds of a cement mixer and an electric
saw.*

SPEER. It was the worst place I had ever seen.

Pause.

It was code-named Dora. It was the plant that made the V-2
rocket, built in caves and tunnels in the Harz Mountains.
It was worked by prisoners from a nearby concentration
camp. Which had of course all kinds of security advantages.

I visited in December 1943. The condition of the prisoners
was utterly . . . well, the word barbaric is . . . Typhoid was
rampant. The prisoners were quartered there, in the sodden,
caves, and of course mortality was extremely high. Not least
because . . . their 'rations' were rancid slop. And the
sanitary arrangements . . . There were these barrels, with
planks, they had to sit on, literally on top . . . and of course,
from time to time, apparently, they'd slip and fall into . . .
And of course, the *smell* . . .

As the vision fades, SPEER *is tottering.*

So, what? Did I 'imagine'?

CASALIS. And that was in December 1943? And you fell ill in
January?

SPEER *collapses.* WOLTERS *and* ANNEMARIE *rush in to
him. As, helped by* ORDERLIES, *they take him out,*
CASALIS *turns to the entering* MARGRET.

1.10.2   Hohenlychen Hospital, February 1944

MARGRET *and Dr Professor Friedrich* KOCH, *with* NURSES, *looking down on* SPEER*'s hospital bed. An* SS-MAN *stands in the corridor.*

MARGRET. Herr Doctor, how is my husband?

KOCH. Well, his temperature and pulse are very high.

MARGRIT. He's spitting blood?

KOCH. He's haemorrhaging, yes.

MARGRIT. So this is not what Himmler's doctor diagnosed? This is not 'rheumatism'?

KOCH. Frau Speer, your husband is extremely ill.

MARGRET. Will he survive?

KOCH. His temperature has stabilised.

Slight pause.

Yes, I think, now, that he will survive.

Pause. MARGRET *breathes deeply. Then she recovers.*

KOCH. Frau Speer. In the midst of . . . the crisis which we hope has passed . . . Your husband looked up to me, quite suddenly and said: 'I've never been so happy'.

1.10.3   Spandau, 1947-1950

KOCH, MARGRET *and the* NURSES *still looking down on* SPEER*'s bed.* SPEER, *standing watching, turns to* CASALIS *when he speaks.*

CASALIS. Do you remember saying that?

SPEER. No, but I remember feeling . . . no.

CASALIS. What do you remember feeling?

SPEER. Things which I fear you would respond to with a healthy scepticism. As did my wife.

CASALIS. Try me.

Pause. During this the group round the bed gradually turn to look at SPEER.

SPEER. Well, apparently, it's fairly common. It was on the worst night, in the hospital, when my temperature and pulse were God knows what, I was haemorrhaging, my skin was blue. And I was suddenly above myself, and looking down, and seeing everything so clearly . . . the doctors and the nurses, hovering, my wife, looking soft and slim, quite beautiful . . . and the ceiling, which was plain and white, was suddenly magnificently ornate, like a mediaeval castle, like indeed the mediaeval castles which my colleagues had so lovingly restored . . . And feeling, yes, that I had never been so happy in my life. But then quite clearly . . . and for me, then, sternly and implacably, I heard two words. 'Not yet'.

Slight pause.

You don't believe me.

CASALIS. I believe that's what you remember.

SPEER *a little laugh. The hospital scene breaks up behind him.*

And I believe that your illness was the result of things outside you.

SPEER. Herr Pastor, my illness began with the recurrence of a knee injury, on a Christmas trip to Lapland.

CASALIS. Your wife thought you were wrongly diagnosed.

SPEER. I was. And then I was correctly diagnosed.

CASALIS. And other people feared you had been poisoned.

SPEER. Herr Hess believes he's being poisoned every day.

CASALIS. But nevertheless. You nearly died.

SPEER. And nevertheless, recovered.

CASALIS. And when you had recovered, changed?

Pause.

SPEER. You are trying to connect my illness with the things I'd seen. Of course, I understand. It is the fashion of the age.

Slight pause.

And yes, things changed. But the change did not originate with me.

1.10.4   Klessheim Castle, 19 March 1944

HITLER *enters to* SPEER, *who sits in a wheelchair in a dressing gown with a blanket over his knees.* MARGRET *there.*

HITLER. My dear Speer, how are you?

SPEER (*to* CASALIS). He was in Austria for a conference with the Hungarians.

HITLER. I am delighted that you are recovered.

SPEER. As ever, he kissed my wife's hand.

HITLER *kisses* MARGRET*'s hand.*

HITLER. Now you see, what I have always told your husband, dear Frau Speer. It is this love of sliding down the sides of mountains in the snow. These long boards on your feet – it's madness! In the fire with them! Please assure me, Speer, you will throw them all away!

HITLER *holds out his hand.* SPEER *does not take it, but speaks again to* CASALIS.

SPEER. And it was his face.

HITLER. And I believe . . . it is your birthday?

SPEER. And I looked at him – his sallow skin, his ugly nose, and thought – how could I not have seen?

HITLER *smiles, pats* SPEER*'s arm.*

HITLER. Well, then. Well, there it is. Well done.

> HITLER *and* MARGRET *go out.* SPEER *stands, takes off his dressing gown, puts on his overcoat.*

SPEER. And for the first time, the magic hadn't worked. And I thought: who is this man, who had meant so much to me?

CASALIS. So this was – essentially aesthetic?

SPEER. It was the moment that I realised – he'd changed. That he'd betrayed those great ideals with which he had inspired us all.

CASALIS. And you don't think that this was connected \ with the labourers –

SPEER. With the workmen in the mountains? No. I wish it was. Mine was not a moral opposition. It was because from that point on – as the Russians, British and Americans closed in on us – he extended his intentions to *my* area of responsibility.

> *We begin to sense the firework display of a distant air-raid, coming closer.*

And I finally realised that he intended to pull the German people down into perdition with him. That far from saving it, he was preparing to destroy his Fatherland.

And worst of all that there were people – good people, friends – prepared to let him drag them down.

1.11   The Town Hall, Breslau, late January 1945

The air-raid continues. Enter HANKE *to* SPEER.

HANKE. Speer. Welcome.

SPEER. Hanke, my dear friend. This is so beautiful.

HANKE. We begin by refurbishing a Karl Friedrich Schinkel building on the Wilhemsplatz, all those years ago. And we end destroying one in Breslau.

Looking out.

Well, if the Americans don't do it first.

SPEER. 'Destroy'?

HANKE. The order is quite clear. Monuments. And palaces, castles, telephone exchanges. Theatres, opera houses, industrial plants. I have it pinned up on every noticeboard.

SPEER. What, alongside 'every man need only know what is going on in his domain'?

HANKE. So you think the war is lost?

SPEER. But if it isn't lost . . . then why destroy what we must recapture?

Pause.

HANKE. 'The enemy will be defeated by weapons that are superior to his'.

SPEER. I have told Goebbels he must stop promising ultimate salvation through miracle weapons which do not exist. We must face up to what is happening and not destroy our people's vital means of life.

HANKE. And leave a perfect Schinkel building to be trashed by the Red Army?

SPEER. I believe that beauty is a vital means of life. And we have to stick to not destroying it, whatever we have to face up to, in the future.

HANKE. Sometimes I wonder – if the Führer only knew . . .

SPEER. Oh, Karl. My friend.

A moment.

HANKE (*gesturing around him*). All right. For you. I'll leave your precious Schinkel standing. Prove your point.

Pause. The bombing very loud, the explosions lighting up the sky.

SPEER. My friend. Your name will live in the German Pantheon forever. You are going to a fine and worthy end.

HANKE. You know, there is a kind of . . . dreadful beauty in all this.

SPEER. I know. As does the Führer.

HANKE *looks at* SPEER, *then turns and goes quickly out.* SPEER *turns to* CASALIS.

SPEER. But it got worse. On the 19th of March Hitler issued another decree, ordering the physical destruction of all German industry, and the forcible evacuation of the German population in the west ahead of the advancing American and British armies. And so whatever the risks to me and to my family, I knew I had to go back to the ruined Chancellory to make one final effort to persuade him to relent.

1.12.1   The Bunker, 29 March 1945

SPEER *turns to see* FRÄULEIN WOLF, *hurrying along a corridor in the bunker. She is not pleased to see* SPEER.

SPEER. Ah, Wolf, I have a document for \ the Führer –

FRAULEIN WOLF. He has your document, Herr Speer.

SPEER. Reichsminister. This is another document, I want you to type up on the 12 point typewriter . . .

FRÄULEIN WOLF. I can't, Reichsminister.

SPEER. Whyever not?

FRÄULEIN WOLF. I have been ordered not to.

She hurries on. SCHAUB *appears.*

SCHAUB. Follow me.

SPEER. And so I was led along the narrow corridors, surrounded as I knew by walls 3.6 metre thick, beneath the five metre, solid concrete roof, to the room where he awaited me.

1.12.2   The Bunker, 29 March 1945

The room where the pieces of the Germania model are now kept. SPEER *enters to* HITLER, *who sits on the base of the great domed hall, holding a document.*

HITLER. Well, Herr Speer, you see that despite the efforts of the enemy above us we may still converse surrounded by your architecture.

SPEER *nods graciously.* HITLER *puts on his spectacles.*

An irony, in view of your defection to the ranks of the whiners and fainthearts.

SPEER. Um \ may I ask –

HITLER. Yes, here it all is, your report, the usual stuff . . . Final collapse of the German war economy . . . war cannot continue on the military plane . . . our obligation to maintain the people's means of life . . . We have no right, it is not our duty, no one can take the viewpoint that the fate of the German people as a whole is tied to his fate personally.

He takes his spectacles off and glares at SPEER.

SPEER. My Führer. I am merely echoing what you yourself said so eloquently in *Mein Kampf* . . .

HITLER. You haven't read *Mein Kampf.*

SPEER. You will not wish me to deceive you.

HITLER. It is not a matter of what you say to me. I am told that you have told the Ruhr Gauleiters that the war is lost. Are you aware that that is treason? And what measures I would have to take? If you were not my architect?

SPEER. My Führer you must act as you think fit. Without consideration for my person.

Pause.

HITLER. I must act 'without consideration for your person'.

A sudden change of tack.

Speer, you have worked too hard. You should take some leave.

SPEER. No, my Führer. I am fit and well. If you want to get rid of me, you must dismiss me.

HITLER. You know I can't do that.

SPEER. Nor can I remain the Minister in name if I desert my post.

Pause. HITLER *doesn't know what to do. He sits and looks away.* SPEER *sits.*

HITLER. All right.

Pause.

You know, in some ways the enemy's advance is a great help to us. People fight fanatically when they have the war at their front door.

SPEER. My Führer, as I pointed out in my memorandum the enemy's military superiority \ means that –

HITLER. I sometimes think, the luck. I was always lucky. And then that dreadful early winter in 1941. And the allies get blue skies for Normandy. But, yet, despite all of that, we struggle on, with unshakable determination. You – what – you doubled tank production in two years. You trebled airplanes and munitions. Artillery, quadrupled. When naturally the moaners and whiners said it was impossible.

Pause.

Which is why I will give you one more chance.

SPEER. I'm sorry?

HITLER. If you can assure me that the war can still be won, then you can keep your post.

Pause.

SPEER. My Führer, the war is lost.

HITLER. Or indeed, if you still had faith the war might still be won.

Pause.

Or even . . . that you *hoped* that we aren't lost. At least you could say that. And then I would be satisfied.

SPEER. My Führer, how could I lie to you? It would be like lying to myself.

HITLER *stands.*

HITLER. You think about it. And then let me know.

SPEER. Um . . . 'think about it'?

HITLER. Whether you're prepared to hope the war might still be won.

SPEER. But I . . .

HITLER. You know, when the whiners and the fainthearts say that it's impossible, then I say – look at Speer.

HITLER *hits* SPEER *with the glare. It holds a long time.*

You can say it in your own words. Any way you like.

SPEER *turns away.* HITLER *pleased to have won, but furious that* SPEER *has not done what he asked.*

Well, there it is.

He turns to go. Suddenly.

SPEER. My Führer, how could you doubt me. I stand unconditionally behind you.

HITLER *turns back to* SPEER. *We don't know how he will react. After a long moment, it is* HITLER *who turns away, nodding, his eyes brimming with tears. He comes to* SPEER *putting out his hand.* SPEER *puts out his hand,* HITLER *takes it and converts it into the elbow cupping gesture.*

HITLER. Well. Heil Speer.

SPEER (*pressing his advantage*). My Führer. Will you do one thing for me?

HITLER *looks quizzically at* SPEER.

Will you give me and my ministry sole responsibility for implementing your decree of March 19?

HITLER. For implementing? Not for changing it?

SPEER. For implementing it, my Führer. Absolutely and entirely.

SPEER *takes a paper from his pocket.*

SPEER. It will require a sentence.

HITLER. Yes of course.

SPEER *gives the piece of paper to* HITLER.

Very well.

HITLER *takes the document to a table to sign it.*

A glass of wine?

SPEER. That would be very welcome.

HITLER *calls.*

HITLER. Schaub!

To SPEER, *as he signs.*

My hands are shaking. Lately it's been hard for me to write even a few words.

Enter SCHAUB.

SCHAUB. 'Führer.

HITLER. Schaub, can you have them get a glass of wine for the Reichsminister.

SCHAUB *goes out.* HITLER *stands, turns back to* SPEER.

You know, if the war is lost then the people will be lost, and it is not necessary to worry about their needs. For the garbage left over after this will be only the inferior, as the best are dead. And the future belongs entirely to the hard men of the east.

SPEER. What?

HITLER *hands him the document.*

HITLER. We will leave this world in flame. I am confident in assigning this last duty to my Minister of Armaments.

HITLER *disappears.*

1.12.3   Berlin, 29–30 March 1945

WOLTERS *and* ANNEMARIE *enter to* SPEER. CASALIS *is there.*

ANNEMARIE. Thank God.

SPEER (*handing* WOLTERS *the document* HITLER *signed*). Five thousand copies.

WOLTERS. New orders?

SPEER. Yes. And are \ the vehicles I ordered –

WOLTERS (*reading the document*). Yes, as you ordered.

ANNEMARIE. Cars, trucks, lorries, motorbikes, and bicycles . . .

WOLTERS. . . . standing by.

SPEER. Excellent.

WOLTERS (*reading*). So you got the old man to sign over everything to us.

SPEER. The Führer assigned me this last duty, yes.

WOLTERS. To countermand his general order as and when we think it fit.

SPEER. No.

WOLTERS. But that is what you plan to do.

SPEER. I plan to stop the destruction of the factories and farms and mines on which our people's future life depends.

SPEER *turns to go.*

Where are you going first?

SPEER. East.

WOLTERS. A question.

SPEER. Yes?

WOLTERS. What happens if you turn the corner and run into an enemy patrol?

Slight pause.

SPEER. Oh, I've got that all worked out. It's simple. I'd surround them.

The tension between them is broken. WOLTERS *laughs, turns and goes out.*

CASALIS. And did it work?

SPEER. Yes. It saved German industry.

CASALIS. By betraying Hitler.

SPEER. As he and those who followed his last orders had given up the German people.

CASALIS. So despite your efforts there was destruction?

SPEER. Yes, sadly. For instance, I discovered that despite his pledge Karl Hanke had in fact blown up the Schinkel building. And everything besides. And then escaped from an inferno of his own creation.

CASALIS. Your old friend.

SPEER. Yes.

CASALIS. And so did you see Hitler, once again?

SPEER. Yes, on the 25th of April . . . I flew in and landed on the East-West axis and I was taken down into the bunker, where at approaching midnight I was told I was invited for refreshments.

SCHAUB *enters.*

SCHAUB. Please follow me.

SPEER. And so I did.

1.13.1   Eva Braun's room, bunker, 25 April 1945

SPEER *enters* EVA BRAUN*'s room. She looks rather guilty.*

SPEER. Eva.

EVA BRAUN. Oh good it's you.

She retrieves a lit cigarette she's just hidden.

SPEER. I didn't know you smoked.

EVA BRAUN. Extreme circumstances call for extreme measures. Do you want one?

SPEER. No.

EVA BRAUN. If 'someone' comes in and detects the smell, it's yours. But I bet you'd like some cake and some champagne.

SPEER. You're the first person to think I might be hungry.

EVA BRAUN. Everybody's got things on their minds.

SPEER. As have you.

Pause. She busies herself with cake and wine.

EVA BRAUN. Do you recognise your furniture?

SPEER. Of course.

EVA BRAUN. It too is a comfort to me in these times.

SPEER. I'm pleased.

EVA BRAUN. It's so sad, what's happened to all those lovely rooms upstairs.

SPEER. Yes, it is. But is not the saddest.

EVA BRAUN. Pop!

She pours champagne.

So how's Frau Speer, and all the children?

SPEER. She's very well. I've moved them to a place of safety, in the . . . in the area the British are attacking now.

EVA BRAUN. Good man. D'you want some cake?

SPEER. I saw Goebbels earlier. He appears to think that we can make a separate peace with the British and Americans.

EVA BRAUN (*cutting cake*). Oh, is that right?

SPEER. Well, I'm not sure it's entirely realistic . . .

EVA BRAUN (*handing* SPEER *a piece of cake*). Hey, have you heard the latest?

SPEER. No?

EVA BRAUN (*stubs out her cigarette*). His ministry is putting out fake horoscopes. Do you want a peppermint?

SPEER. Fake *what*?

EVA BRAUN *finds a newspaper.*

EVA BRAUN. Look here, it's true.

She opens the newspaper, pops a peppermint into her mouth.

Now, what are you?

SPEER. Professionally?

EVA BRAUN. Your birth sign, Herr Reichsminister.

SPEER. Well, I was born on March 19.

EVA BRAUN. Ah. Pisces. 'You are going through a term of trial but if you are steadfast and your will remains unshakable you will prevail against all odds'. So what's Frau Speer?

SPEER. Well . . . she's September . . .

EVA BRAUN. Oh, *Albert*.

SPEER (*guessing*). The 28th.

EVA BRAUN. Libra. And yes. Sometimes she must fear she's on the wrong path but nevertheless she will reach her final destination. So – you've done the right thing there.

SPEER. And you?

EVA BRAUN. Well, I'm Aquarius. And although things may look black I must be assured that they who love and care for me are acting always for the best. Isn't it priceless?

Pause. Delicately, she puts her hand on SPEER*'s arm.*

You know he had decided to stay here, and I am staying with him. Like everyone, he wanted me to go to Munich. But I'm happy to be here. And you know the rest, of course.

Slight pause.

So my dear Albert, please, no pestering! I have reached my destination.

SPEER *smiles.* EVA BRAUN *eats another peppermint.*

EVA BRAUN. He was so pleased you came.

SPEER. Yes. Though I fear he would be less pleased if he knew \ what I've been –

EVA BRAUN (*interrupting*). He thought that you had gone against him, like the others.

SPEER. You see, I have been countermanding \ orders to destroy –

EVA BRAUN (*interrupting*). But I know that you will always stand behind him, unconditionally.

Pause.

SPEER. But surely. We must surely, all of us, feel there were things that shouldn't have occurred. Things said or done, or left undone.

EVA BRAUN. You mean, not having children?

Pause.

Well, perhaps. But after all, I am the Mother of the Nation.

SPEER *smiles, a little wanly, giving up.* EVA BRAUN *yawns.*

Well, I must go to bed. And you must go to . . . to your family.

They look at each other.

I told him – Speer will not betray you. Well, my case is proved, I think. Don't you?

SPEER *says nothing.* EVA BRAUN *puts her hand out to* SPEER.

EVA BRAUN. Well. So long.

SPEER. So long.

She shakes his hand. SPEER *turns and goes out of the room.*

1.13.2   Corridor, bunker, 25 April 1945

SPEER *meets* HITLER, *looking at a map, and* VON BELOW.

SPEER. Heil, my Führer.

HITLER. Ah, Speer, you're leaving?

SPEER. Yes, my Führer.

HITLER. Ah.

> HITLER *looks at* SPEER. *For a moment, the same, blinding look.*

HITLER. Well, then. Well, there it is. Goodbye.

> *To* VON BELOW.

> Will you get Keitel? If we're going to split the two commands, then we must do it now, while there's still a corridor . . .

> HITLER *goes out with* VON BELOW *following.*

1.14.1   Hamburg, 1 May 1945

SPEER *turns to* CASALIS, *as* ANNEMARIE *enters with a small bag. She opens the bag, takes out a red leather case, opens it, sets up a picture of Hitler in a silver frame. As* SPEER *takes off his coat:*

SPEER. So that was it. No wishes to my family, no . . . statement, affirmation. No good luck. Nothing beyond . . . goodbye. And he was gone.

And so I went north, to join Dönitz, who was trying to negotiate surrender with the British. I was assigned a small room in a navy barracks. Frau Kempf had packed a small overnight bag for me, in which she'd put a portrait photograph of the Führer, in a silver frame, which he had given me six weeks before.

ANNEMARIE *goes out with the jacket.* SPEER *goes and looks at the picture.*

CASALIS. And presumably that's where you heard about his death?

SPEER *can't answer. He nods.*

And may I ask – what did you feel?

SPEER *says nothing. Instead he starts to sob. He can't stop it, it goes on and on, until he is literally too exhausted to sob any more. He looks to* CASALIS.

SPEER. I felt that I was free of him at last.

1.14.2   Spandau, 1950

CASALIS. You felt that you were free of him? At last?

SPEER *a little wearily, taking his prison jacket from the case and putting it on:*

SPEER. I've said. I realised too late.

CASALIS. Of course. You were an expert, not a politician.

SPEER. Yes.

CASALIS. You had sought where possible to improve the conditions of your workers.

SPEER. Yes.

CASALIS. You had visited one concentration camp.

SPEER. Yes.

CASALIS. You were ignorant of a systematic plan \ to murder –

SPEER. Yes.

CASALIS. But what do you think you would have done, if you *had* known?

Pause.

SPEER. This is of course the question. And the answer doesn't help me sleep at night. I fear I would have said: 'You're killing them? But that's insane. I need them for my factories'.

That is why I came to you, and asked you to help me to become a different man. And you said you could and would if I told you the truth.

CASALIS. And do you think you have?

SPEER. Why, do you think I've been lying to you all this time?

CASALIS. No, Herr Speer. I don't think you've been lying. But I must tell you the questions that remain. You have told me you were let down by this man who had promised you so much. But was it really that? Was it not rather a playing out of what was there from the beginning? Is it not the case in truth that the hope was always false because the choice was always wrong? That there was a straight line from your building of the new Berlin to the blasting of that tunnel by those miserable slave-workers in the mountain. That the granite for Germania was quarried by the inmates of Mauthausen. That the searchlights which obscured the stomachs of the party bureaucrats at Nuremberg also blinded you to what was being thought and said and planned. Herr Speer, you have presented me the story of a man who was inspired by great ideals and saw those great ideals betrayed. And yet. I see a man with all the intellectual, yes, and all the moral strength to have seen through all of this. Surely, when you look back to the first time when you looked into those eyes, don't you ask yourself, how in God's name was I taken in by that?

SPEER *is appalled.*

SPEER. Look, Pastor. You had a simple war. Dangerous of course. Unenviable in many ways. But simple in that in hindsight there's no doubt at all that you were right. Now

put yourself in my shoes. Ask yourself what hindsight asks
of me. Had I done what was required of me by posterity in
the war I would have been shot by Hitler. Had I admitted
what I was asked to admit after the war, I would have
hanged at Nuremberg. My crime consisted of not knowing
and not asking what I didn't know, about an evil we will
perish if we do not understand. For that – I have been
condemned as a war criminal, robbed of my freedom,
tortured with the knowledge that I based my life upon a
catastrophic error. If you demand of me that I should have
done more than I did, then you must be sure that if – God
forbid – it came to that for you, you would make and meet
the same demands on yourself. Till then . . . I must repeat.
I could have known, I should have known. I didn't know.
I was blinded by what I felt about him at the start to what
he reall – . . . To what he had become.

CASALIS. But still, you see, you cannot say: 'to what he
really always was'.

CASALIS *realises he has gone too far.*

I'm sorry. I should not have . . . It is not my job to judge \
or to cross-examine you –

SPEER. So what *is* your job? If it is not 'to judge to probe and
to interrogate'.

CASALIS. It is to repeat those two words. To a man who
thought he should have died at Nuremberg.

SPEER. What words?

CASALIS. 'Not yet'. To a man who now may have begun to
live.

SPEER. Begun?

CASALIS. Like his garden here in Spandau, he has cleared the
undergrowth. Now the time has come to plant new seeds in
fresh soil.

Enter HESS *with a chair.*

HESS. Ah. There you are.

SPEER. Herr Hess?

HESS. I've something for you.

SPEFR. Yes?

HESS. I broke my chair. You lent me yours.

SPEER. I did.

HESS. I understand you take your chair to religious service every Sunday. So you will have need of it. I mended mine. The whole thing's mumbo-jumbo, anyway.

He goes out, leaving the chair.

SPEER. In fact it is not my chair. It's Neurath's. It was found for him to help his back. But oddly enough, it is my chair in another sense. In that it was my own design.

Pause.

CASALIS. Well.

SPEER. Herr Pastor, God preserve your strength.

CASALIS. And yours. Please – stay. You have your chair.

CASALIS *goes.* SPEER *turns out front.*

SPEER. And he was gone. To complete his doctorate at Strasbourg.

Pause.

I said that when I heard of Hitler's death I felt that I was free of him at last. But as you know that isn't true at all.

Yes. Yes. That's when the dreams began.

Dreams of his knowing what I did, dreams of his knowing what I thought.

And I realised he wasn't really dead at all.

1.15.1   Germany

SPEER *is dreaming. Suddenly, the sky is full of fire. Through it walks* VON BELOW.

VON BELOW. In October 1942, I was approached by a young lieutenant of the communications corps, who'd been working on a cable transfer somewhere in the Ukraine. He'd come upon a troop of SS shooting men and women in a trench.

I naturally investigated this. I was advised that this was not a matter of concern for me.

Now the fire feels like the torches of the Nuremberg rallies. Enter GANZENMÜLLER.

GANZENMÜLLER. On the 28th of July 1942, yes, I appear to have signed a letter to SS General Wolff. 'With reference to our telephone conversation of 16th July, I am able to inform you that since 22 July one train a day, with 5,000 Jews, is going from Warsaw to Treblinka . . . '

Now the torches are topped by Speer's Cathedral of Light, through which walks HANKE.

HANKE. All right. I'm going to say this once – and you're going to say nothing. There's a place, in Upper Silesia, on the Vistula near Crakow.

It's vast, goes on for ever. I.G. Farben has a plant there. In the Polish it's Oswiecem and we call it Auschwitz. And if you're invited there – don't go. I can't describe it. I am not permitted to describe it. Just don't go.

1.15.2   Posen, 1943

Then the light becomes candelabra in the darkness and a small man enters, now alone, to a lectern. Finding it hard to see through the gothic gloom, he blinks, and cleans his glasses. Then he begins.

HIMMLER. I want to speak now, in this most restricted circle, about a matter which you, my party comrades, have long accepted as a matter of course, but which for me has become the heaviest burden of my life – the matter of the Jews.

The brief sentence 'The Jews must be exterminated' is easy to pronounce, but the demands on those who have to put it into practice are the hardest and the most difficult in the world.

We, you see, were faced with the question 'What about the women and children?' And I decided, here too, to find an unequivocal solution. For I did not think that I was justified in exterminating – meaning kill or order to have killed – the men, but to leave their children to grow up to take revenge on our sons and grandchildren.

For the organisation which had to carry out this order, it was the most difficult one we were ever given. I think I can say that it has been carried out without damaging the minds and spirits of our men, or of our leaders.

Blackout.

End of Act One.

ACT TWO

'People cannot find a place in their imagination
(or allow themselves to remember) unimaginable horror.
It is possible to live in a twilight between knowing
and not knowing'.

W.A.Visser 't Hooft, Dutch theologian
(quoted in Gitta Sereny, *Albert Speer: His Battle with Truth*)

ACT TWO

2.1.1 Spandau Garden, August 1966 and September 1954

A bench on one side. On the other, SPEER kneels, looking down. We might think he is praying, or in a state of abject misery. In fact, he is planting a flower with a trowel. He looks up. He is 60 years old.

SPEER wears a corduroy prison suit stamped with the number five on the breast, back and knees. He stands and speaks.

SPEER. So who is this old man? Well, he was first an architect, whose works proclaimed his country's power to the world. And then a Minister, building armaments to dominate the world. But now he is a gardener . . . who built a place of beauty in the midst of all the dust and rubble, which he pretended was the world.

Who is he? Well, he's all these things. But most importantly, he is your father.

HESS enters. He is in his 60s, as he was in 1954. His corduroy uniform is stamped four.

It was Herr Hess who gave me the idea.

HESS sits on the garden bench.

So how are you today, Herr Hess?

HESS. Oh, pretty bad.

SPEER (*out front*). He was Hitler's deputy. And frankly he'd been pretty screwy even then.

HESS. However. I've decided I was wrong to think my food was being doctored to give me stomach cramps. After all, I can take any one of the seven bowls that are standing on the table.

SPEER. So you've got over your obsession.

HESS. Oh, no. That would never do. If I got over it, it wouldn't be obsessive.

SPEER *looks at* HESS, *fascinated by this logic.*

SPEER. We all have our eccentricities. Do you know that I'm collecting kilometres? Don't you think that's crazy, writing down the distances I've walked each day?

HESS. Why not, if you enjoy it?

SPEER. But every week, I add them up, and calculate the weekly average, and enter the results.

HESS *shrugs.*

And even to start off I had to calculate my walking course, by measuring my foot, 31 centimetres, then walking heel to toe, 870 times, to work out my track.

HESS. Sounds logical to me.

SPEER. But it gets worse. Now I plan to walk to Heidelberg! 616 kilometres! That's Two Thousand Three Hundred and eighteen point fifty two circuits of my track! Isn't this completely mad?

HESS. Well only if \ you want to –

SPEER. And the worst thing is, my real obsession is that I'll miscount and get there late. Can you believe that? That I could have been sitting in my favourite pastry shop but I'm still trudging through the outskirts in the rain!

HESS *stands and goes out.*

Herr Hess? Have I offended you?

HESS *returns with a tin.*

HESS. Here. Take 30 beans. Put them in your left pocket. Then every round drop one into your right pocket. And at night you count them up. You understand?

SPEER. Yes. Thank you, Hess.

HESS. Don't mention it.

He makes to go.

A thought. Why stop at Heidelberg?

HESS *goes out.*

2.1.2   Spandau Garden, August 1966

SPEER *turns out front.*

SPEER. And so from Heidelberg I walked to Munich. Then across the mountains to Vienna. And all the time, I was thinking, when I got back to my cell, and found a scrap of paper, what I'd write to little or as time passed not so little Hilde.

When you were young, about how I first met your mother, and some jokey stories about life in prison in my 'magazine' for you, the Spanish Illustrated. Then later, when I made our secret rule: that if something's wrong, but you don't want to say so, then put the word 'nevertheless' before the sentence. Thus if you say, 'Nevertheless, I'm fine', it means you are not fine at all. Meanwhile, I walk on. My record for one day so far is 24.7 kilometres, my best pace 5.8 kilometres an hour. To aid me, the person who I call 'my friend' has obtained for me by our secret channel maps, travelogues, art history . . . he warns me of all natural barriers, raging rivers, glaciers, mountains, and sends me descriptions of the wonders I will pass.

You ask about the Nazis. You say how could an intelligent person go along with such a thing.

This morning I left Europe and crossed the pontoon bridge to Asia. I have trouble picturing the magnificent panorama: mosques and minarets in the midst of a tangle of small houses. How many towers does Hagia Sofia have?

To reassure you: of the dreadful things, I knew nothing. As far as practising anti-semitism or even uttering anti-Semitic remarks, my conscience is entirely clear. I really had no aversion to them, or rather, no more than the slight discomfort all of us sometimes feel when in contact with these people . . .

And today I am 353 kilometres from Kabul. If no snowstorms intervene I should be there mid-January.

Already we are fewer: three years ago Neurath was released, a year later Raeder and last year Dönitz. And Neurath died.

Now there are only 780 kilometres to Calcutta, which will mark the completion of my ten thousandth kilometre.

And I wonder: will I later miss these quiet days with books and gardening, free from ambition and vexation? When I'm released, will I still be able to cope with the world?

Funk was released two years ago and now he too has died.

For more than a year now I've been tramping north through endless woods of larch and fir, with gnarled silver birches in the highlands.

And now another 500 kilometres through the snowy wastes to the Bering Straight still lie before me, all to be done in almost total darkness. However, wonderful northern lights, such as I saw in Lapland at the end of 1943, continually transform the scenery.

HESS *enters. He is now in his late 70s.*

The strait is frozen till mid March. I wanted to arrive in time to walk across. And so I have.

HESS. Herr Speer, you are talking to yourself.

SPEER. Yes, indeed I am. And in fact, Herr Hess \ you may be interested –

HESS. Schirach says that in mental hospitals they set the feeble-minded to the gardening.

SPEER. You may be interested to hear \ that you are looking –

HESS. Good point, I think.

SPEER. – that you are looking at the first central European to reach America by foot.

Pause.

HESS. This is more serious than I thought.

SPEER. Clearly you don't remember.

HESS. No.

SPEER. So here's a clue. The word is 'beans'?

HESS. No, it won't do.

SPEER. Don't you remember? The 30 beans, to transfer from one pocket to the other. Look!

He shows HESS *his beans.*

HESS. You mean you've kept it up for all this time?

SPEER. Seventy-eight thousand five hundred and fourteen rounds. Twenty-one thousand two hundred and one kilometres. And look – the Bering Strait. The gateway to Alaska, Canada, Seattle. California!

HESS. Well . . . and they say I'm crazy.

He goes out.

SPEER (*out front*). And so. Hilde. This is my last letter. And a chance to thank you for all the extraordinary energy and love you expended in the effort to shorten my time here . . . the love from you to me was always the greatest gift.

SPEER *stands a moment, then, in a different tone:*

And what I thought but didn't say . . . This idiotic organisation of emptiness . . . What I am left with in the end is nothing but the foolish satisfaction of having marched obstinately in a circle for decades.

Through a mirrored hall of hundreds of unchanging faces, over and over, and all mine.

You know, if I had lived fully here, I think I would have had to die. Instead, I have become the man I never was.

*He reaches into his sock and takes out a scrap of
cardboard, from which he reads:*

A telegram. To 'my friend'. Rudi. This should reach you at
precisely midnight, 30 September 1966. Please pick me up
35 kilometres south of Guadalajara, Mexico.

2.2.1   Outside Spandau. Midnight, 30 September 1966

Midnight chimes. SPEER *walks out of Spandau, surrounded by
British* GUARDS, *into the chaos of a phalanx of* PRESSMEN,
film and TV cameras, flashbulbs. On the edge of the crush is
SPEER's *lawyer* FLACHSNER, *66, leading* MARGRET
towards her husband. Rudi WOLTERS *is on the edge of the
scene.*

PRESSMEN (*variously*). Herr Speer, how does it feel to be
released?

What do you think of the treatment you received?

This way please, Herr Speer!

What are your plans?

FLACHSNER. Excuse me, excuse me please –

PRESSMEN. Frau Speer, how long is it since you've seen your
husband?

Just turn your head this way, Frau Speer!

Do you think your sentence was just?

Where are you going now, sir?

Have you changed your views on Hitler?

Do you think you have paid a proper price?

Are you happy with your treatment in Spandau?

What was your view about the Eichmann trial?

FLACHSNER *and* MARGRET *have reached* SPEER, *who
looks happy but bewildered. They shake hands.*

FLACHSNER *is holding up his hands trying to stop the barrage of questions so that he and* SPEER *can speak.*

PRESSMEN. What did you most miss in prison?

What do you think about the Berlin wall?

How were your relations with your fellow prisoners?

Please look over here, Herr Speer!

SPEER *holds up his hands along with* FLACHSNER *and the hubbub dissolves into silence.*

PRESSMEN. Why were you not released early?

Do you feel responsible for Nazi crimes?

Do you think you were unjustly treated?

Do you think you've paid the price?

FLACHSNER. Ladies and gentlemen. Herr Speer will make a short statement.

FIRST PRESSMAN. What are your immediate plans?

SPEER. Ladies and gentlemen, may I say at first that I am quite glad to be out.

Laughter. The beginnings of questions, which SPEER *stops with a gesture.*

PRESSMEN. Do you plan to go back to architecture, Herr Speer?

SPEER. You will understand that I can only be brief tonight, for this evening belongs to my wife.

HECKLER. It's not your business to say anything!

Booing and shhing.

SPEER. So you will forgive me for answering your questions this way. My sentence was just. I was treated correctly at all times. I have no complaints. Thank you so much.

FIRST PRESSMAN. What are your plans, Herr Speer?

SPEER. My immediate plans are to spend some quiet days with my family.

SECOND PRESSMAN. And beyond?

SPEER. I am an architect –

HECKLER. Architect!

SPEER. – and I hope to find people who will let me practise my profession. Thank you very much.

THIRD PRESSMAN. Herr Speer, do you think you have paid the price for what you did?

SPEER. And now please, everyone . . .

FLACHSNER *pushing through the* PRESS, *making a path for* SPEER *and* MARGRET *to the car.*

FLACHSNER. Thank you, that's all.

3RD PRESSMAN. Will you be giving further interviews, Herr Speer?

FLACHSNER. No, he will not.

PRESSMEN. What is your view about the Frankfurt trials?

Do you plan to meet with any world leaders?

Will there be a press conference?

FLACHSNER. There are no further questions. Herr and Frau Speer are going to a private address.

SPEER *passes* WOLTERS.

WOLTERS. So here I am. Just south of Guadalajara.

SPEER. Rudi. Long time no see.

WOLTERS. You will come and see me.

SPEER. Oh, of course.

WOLTERS. I have the ham. And the Johannisberger.

SPEER(*overwhelmed*). And everything you've done for me. For us. For all these years.

WOLTERS. But tonight is for your wife. Go, go.

After this private moment, WOLTERS *is swallowed up by the crowd.*

PRESSMEN. Where are you going, Herr Speer?

Are you going to write about your experiences?

Have you sold your story to a newspaper or magazine?

What is your view on denazification?

What was your relationship with Rudolf Hess?

Will you be meeting up with your old comrades?

The price, Herr Speer! Do you think you've paid the price?

2.2.2   Hunting Lodge, Schleswig-Holstein, 1 October 1966

The SPEER CHILDREN, *their* SPOUSES *and* ANNEMARIE *waiting in a hunting lodge hired by the* SPEERS. *Old fashioned comfort. Downstage, easy chairs and a gramophone. To one side, a table laid for dinner.* HILDE (*30*), *her husband* ULF *Schramm,* ALBERT (*32*), *and his wife* RUTH, FRITZ (*29*) *and* ARNOLD (*26*). *Two* WAITRESSES *stand close to waiting trays of canapés and drinks. The scene starts in silence.* ALBERT *goes and takes a canapé.*

ALBERT. What's this?

FIRST WAITRESS. Paté de fois gras, sir.

HILDE. It was one of the requests.

RUTH. Is that the stuff they make by \ forcefeeding –

ARNOLD. Yes.

ALBERT (*eating*). It's actually quite \ palatable –

ARNOLD. It just tends to be a little rich.

ALBERT gestures anyone to take one.

ALBERT. Paté de fois gras, anyone? Aunt Annemarie?

No one takes up the offer. ANNEMARIE *shakes her head.* HILDE *goes and takes a drink and sits.*

HILDE. Well, as I say, he ordered it.

ULF. He ordered everything.

HILDE. It's been driving us all bonkers. Lists lists lists.

ULF. Appointed tasks.

ALBERT. But after twenty years, I guess you are entitled.

FRITZ. So everybody: best \ behaviour –

A door opens, HILDE *leaps up. Enter the 28-year-old* MARGRET, *her husband* HANS STRAUSS, *and 23-year-old* ERNST.

ALBERT. Margret.

MARGRET JNR. We met Ernst at the station.

HANS. Sorry we're so late.

ARNOLD. It's fine. The old man's not here yet.

ALBERT. Now, Hans, you've met Aunt Annemarie? Who was Father's secretary in the war.

HANS. Of course I have.

HILDE. And truth be told . . .

ANNEMARIE. Ernst! Aren't you looking well.

ERNST JNR. Aha. That's what you get for being over 21.

ARNOLD. Why's that?

ERNST JNR. People stop saying 'aren't you tall'.

RUTH. And haven't started saying 'aren't you old'.

Pause.

HILDE. Of course, you haven't seen him for twenty years.

ANNEMARIE. Not since Nuremberg. And visa versa, naturally.

MARGRET JNR. You look as wonderful as ever.

ALBERT. And in fact \ I think we've all –

FRITZ. In fact, dear family, tarantara, tarantara.

> *Enter* MARGRET *and* SPEER. *Applause.* ALBERT *nods to the* WAITRESSES *who pour champagne into the glasses ready to take them round.*

MARGRET. I'm sorry.

SPEER. We must have . . .

MARGRET. Father thought he spotted a reporter.

SPEER. . . . come round the wrong way.

> *He takes it in.*

> Well. *Well.*

> ALBERT *to him.*

ALBERT. Father, welcome back.

> *They shake hands.*

SPEER. My boy.

ALBERT. And father . . . Ruth.

SPEER. My dear, how wonderful to meet you.

> SPEER *kisses* RUTH*'s hand.*

> You know, your husband has the most lovely hands. Do you remember, Albert, on your first visit, all those years ago?

ALBERT. Of course I do.

SPEER. I shook my son's hand, and I was put up on a charge.

MARGRET. Well, you won't be charged with anything today.

FRITZ. Just charged *for* everything.

HILDE. Fritz! Papa.

SPEER. Hilde, my dearest. And Ulf . . .

MARGRET (*gesturing to* MARGRET JNR). Albert, your daughter.

SPEER. Margret.

MARGRET JNR. Papa.

SPEER. Still, so like my mother.

HANS. And like her mother, sir. I'm Hans Nissen.

SPEER. Of course, of course.

Shakes hands.

And where is little Annagret?

MARGRET JNR. She's in bed, papa! Tomorrow.

SPEER (*turning to* ARNOLD). Of course, of course. Now, Fritz?

ARNOLD. No, Arnold, father.

Pause.

SPEER. Arnold.

ARNOLD. Yes.

SPEER. Ah, well. In jail, your mother sent me photographs I thought were Albert but turned to out to be me as a boy.

This rescues the moment. With a playful if not entirely convincing punch to the shoulder.

So – Arnold.

ARNOLD. Yes. Father, you look marvellous.

SPEER. Well, you're the doctor. Fritz.

Shaking FRITZ's *hand.*

How could I mistake the hell-raiser?

FRITZ. Hell-raiser?

MARGRET. You got drunk – once. I foolishly mentioned in a letter.

FRITZ. Right.

ERNST JNR. And by process of elimination . . .

SPEER. Ernst.

Shakes hands.

It should be easy when you're standing. I marked your
heights up on the wall. As through the years you grew –
grew up from . . .

MARGRET (*rescuing*). Just grew up.

Slight pause.

ANNEMARIE. It's hard to know what to say to someone who
is locked away from you for twenty years.

SPEER *realises it's* ANNEMARIE. *During this* ALBERT
nods to the WAITRESSES, *who bring drinks on trays.*

SPEER. Frau . . . Annemarie.

ANNEMARIE. Albert.

SPEER. For twenty years, I have been just Number Five.

ANNEMARIE. For those who love you, you have never just
been Number Five.

FIRST WAITRESS *offering to* SPEER.

FIRST WAITRESS. Herr Speer.

SPEER. Please, my wife.

FIRST WAITRESS *gives a drink to* MARGRET.

MARGRET. Thank you.

SECOND WAITRESS. A canapé?

SPEER. Aha! Paté de fois gras! I chose it because it's the one
thing everybody likes.

As the drinks and canapés are handed round, SPEER *takes
a canapé and bolts it in one. Then he takes another and
does the same.* ANNEMARIE *notes this undelicate
behaviour.*

FRITZ (*taking a drink*). Well, I suppose, if I'm to live up to
my reputation.

SPEER *nods to* ULF *who surreptitiously produces a small jewellery case.*

MARGRET JNR. Now, father, would you like to sit . . .

ALBERT. Should we move \ into the dining room –

SPEER. Now, I have a duty to perform, in relation to the most important person in the room.

A moment or two while people work out who that is. ULF *gives* SPEER *the case.*

FRITZ. Speech, speech.

SPEER. To thank her, on all your behalfs, for bringing you all up as she has. Which is all the speech she'll get from me.

He hands the case to MARGRET.

MARGRET. Albert, how was this done?

MARGRET *opens the case. It's a gold watch.*

MARGRET. Oh, Albert.

SPEER. It should be engraved.

ULF. It is engraved!

MARGRET (*reads*). 'To his Libra, on his day of Liberation'. *Albert.*

MARGRET JNR. It's beautiful.

ULF. Is it all right?

MARGRET. Of course it is.

ERNST JNR. But mum's not libra. She's a virgo.

Pause.

HILDE. Ernst.

HANS. I'm sure it's right . . .

ERNST JNR. Eighth of September. Virgo.

SPEER. The . . . the eighth.

Pause. ARNOLD *and* ALBERT *look at* HILDE *and* ULF.
HILDE*: 'Nothing to do with me'.* ULF*: 'I did as instructed'.*

MARGRET. Well, all I can say is that I am personally
delighted that your father of all people can make a mistake
with numbers.

Rescue successful.

And I feel that everyone should go through and enjoy what
Fritz reminds us is a most expensive dinner.

HILDE. Yes.

The party proceeds to the table for dinner.

RUTH. What are your plans for the immediate future, Herr
Speer?

SPEER. Well, I have many old acquaintances to renew. As Aunt
Annemarie knows, my friend Rudi Wolters has promised
me a Westphalian ham and a bottle of Johannisberger 37.

MARGRET. I think the places are all marked.

SPEER. It will be strange, we two old codgers meeting after
all this time. He's very fond of all the children.

HILDE. 'Fond' is an understatement!

Everyone is seated.

SPEER. Yes indeed. (*To* RUTH.) And then . . .

ALBERT *taps his glass with a spoon,* MARGRET *shaking
her head, but:*

ALBERT. No, Mama, no speech. But just to raise a glass to
welcome Father home. Having been kept from us for twenty
years.

RUTH. Hear hear.

ARNOLD (*raising his glass*). Father!

THE OTHERS (*variously*). To Father. Papa. Albert. Herr
Speer.

SPEER. Well, as is well known, I too am not one for making speeches. And so . . . the feast!

Atmosphere fully restored. EVERYONE *starting to eat.*

RUTH. 'And then'?

SPEER. I'm sorry?

RUTH. You were talking of your plans.

SPEER. Oh yes. I intend to write my memoirs.

Sudden silence.

MARGRET. Memoirs.

SPEER. Yes. My life and deeds in Hitler's Germany!

MARGRET. He told the press he was going to practise as an architect.

SPEER. Well, that was for the press. (*To* RUTH.) Since you raise . . . the matter of the future. (*To* MARGRET.) So what's wrong?

MARGRET There's nothing wrong.

SPEER. That is clearly not the case.

Agonising pause. MARGRET *stands.*

MARGRET. Excuse me, please . . . I'm sorry.

She hurries out.

SPEER. Uh . . .

ANNEMARIE. Oh, Albert.

ANNEMARIE *stands and follows* MARGRET *out. Neither* SPEER *nor anybody else knows what to say.* SPEER *stands and goes into the other room.* ALBERT *makes to follow but* HILDE *goes instead.*

HILDE. Papa, you must see how she feels.

Slight pause.

SPEER. Go on.

HILDE. After twenty years of watching us grow up, and
building our own lives . . . For it to be . . . the only thing
we're known for. To have it all raked up again.

SPEER. 'Raked up again'. I see.

Pause.

In fact, I've made you my literary executor.

HILDE. What? What about Uncle Rudi?

SPEER. I think it's for the best.

Pause.

I am determined. I will write the book. I think I owe it
to the world. And of course I had thought – or hoped, at
least –you would support me.

MARGRET *comes in, followed by* ANNEMARIE.

MARGRET. Albert, I'm sorry. Please. Let's go back into
dinner.

SPEER. Yes. of course.

SPEER *looks back at* HILDE.

HILDE. Papa, of course you have my full support. In anything
you do.

SPEER *looks at* HILDE. *He turns back to* MARGRET, *who
puts out her arm.* SPEER *goes and walks with his wife back
into dinner.* HILDE *to* ANNEMARIE:

Nevertheless . . .

2.2.3   Germany, late 1970s

ANNEMARIE *out front:*

ANNEMARIE. And of course the problem was: for him, it had
never really been a real family. He hardly knew them in the
war. And being locked away from them for twenty years . . .
But it was also the family in which he had grown up: his

father stopping him pursuing the career he wanted to, his mother such a snob, having to wed in secret because they disapproved of Margret's social class, the intolerable pressure over Ernst at Stalingrad . . .

And so how was he to know what it was like to be a real father? How could he understand they had their own lives and their own concerns? How could he know they wouldn't – couldn't – welcome him as he imagined, unconditionally, with open arms?

2.3.1   Germany, 1970

A publisher's party, in the garden of their offices. Suddenly, the stage is flooded with PARTYGOERS: *in addition to fashionable* YOUNG PEOPLE *in bright late-60s summer clothes* (*and even possibly some* CHILDREN), *they include Wolf-Jobst* SIEDLER (*Speer's publisher*), MARGRET *Speer and Nicholas and Maria* VON BELOW, *and* SPEER *himself. A table piled high with copies of* SPEER's Reminiscences (Inside the Third Reich *in English*), *with another table next to it for him to sign. A microphone on a stand.*

Drinks and cocktail bits are taken round by staff in casual clothes. Everything is easy, informal, contemporary, assured . . . in marked contrast to the nervous stuffiness of the previous scene. SIEDLER *moves immediately to make a speech.*

SIEDLER. Ladies and gentlemen . . .

As always, the volume is wrong but it is quickly and effectively sorted.

Ladies and gentlemen, a moment, your attention. Ullstein is . . . well, moderately proud to welcome almost all of you to its summer party. And of course our guest of honour.

Smattering of applause.

As many people know, particularly in the accounts department, his reminiscences were intended to be a modest success with a long shelf-life in a slow-burn market. I think it is fair to say we failed in this.

Laughter.

We did not intend to sell half a million hardback copies, nor the serial rights to *Die Welt* for 600,000 marks, nor to clean up Europe and then north America in paperback. Through all of this, I've asked myself, how could this thing have gone so wrong?

Laughter.

Clearly we underestimated our new author.

Applause.

And also the importance of his mission, which was to speak, now, a quarter of a century on, not to his own generation but the new generation of young democratic Germans, neither traumatised by guilt nor tortured by denial. To the generation of his children.

He looks around.

Necessarily but bravely honest about that tragic period and his role in it. Herr Albert Speer.

SPEER *comes to the microphone.*

SPEER. Well, I am not one for making speeches.

The usual laughter and calls of 'shame' and 'go on'.

And although there is a perfectly good story illustrating this . . . I am advised by Herr Siedler to point out that you may read it on page 217.

Laughter.

All I will say is to thank Herr Sidler for all his efforts with I fear an often recalcitrant new author. Thank you.

Applause. SIEDLER *back to the microphone a moment.*

SIEDLER. And I believe Herr Speer – who is not recalcitrant at all, will sign copies which we happen by coincidence to have available for purchase here this very afternoon.

The formality breaks. SPEER *is escorted by a* YOUNG WOMAN *to his table.* MARGRET *meets the* VON BELOWS.

MARGRET. Well, Klaus. How good of you to come.

VON BELOW. Margret.

MARGRET (*kissing* FRAU VON BELOW). Maria.

   SIEDLER *working his way over.*

VON BELOW. He's looking marvellous.

FRAU VON BELOW. You both are.

MARGRET. He'll be delighted that you're here. He speaks so
   warmly of the help you gave him with the book.

VON BELOW (*demurring*). Well . . .

MARGRET. Help that I fear I was unable . . .

FRAU VON BELOW. Well, of course, it all looks different in
   retrospect. I mean, those evenings at the Berghof with the
   Chief were not quite so boring at the time.

   SIEDLER *arrives.*

SIEDLER. Klaus, Frau von Below, I'm so pleased you could
   come. It's my aim to persuade your husband to follow in
   Herr Speer's footsteps.

FRAU VON BELOW. Really?

SIEDLER. Please, let me introduce you to our chairman.

   SIEDLER *moves off with the* VON BELOWS, *leaving*
   MARGRET *standing for a moment alone. Meanwhile,*
   SPEER *is signing books. His current customer we will know*
   later as MRS WINTERINGHAM.

SPEER. Who shall I write it to?

MRS WINTERINGHAM. To Trudi.

SPEER. Ah.

   He signs, hands the book over.

MRS WINTERINGHAM. Thank you, Herr Speer.

   SPEER *takes the book from the next in line.*

SPEER. Thank you. How would you like this signed?

WOLTERS. Oh, I think, 'to Rudi' would be fine, don't you?

SPEER *looks up.*

SPEER. Rudi. You're here.

WOLTERS. Well, you know what they say, about Mohammed and the Mountain.

SIEDLER *arrives.*

SIEDLER. Now, I hope we're not exploiting you too grossly . . .

SPEER. Herr Siedler, this is Rudolf Wolters.

SIEDLER. Ah. 'My friend'.

WOLTERS. And erstwhile literary executor.

Slight pause.

SIEDLER. Um . . .

WOLTERS. Albert I need a word with you.

SPEER *looks at* SIEDLER.

SIEDLER. Of course.

To the queue.

A moment, and Herr Speer will return.

He leads SPEER *and* WOLTERS *to the building.*

2.4.1   Germany, 1970

Continuous: a room inside the publisher's building. SIEDLER *leaves* SPEER *and* WOLTERS.

WOLTERS. Well, congratulations Herr Reichsminister.

SPEER. Rudi, it's good to see you.

WOLTERS. Thank God you didn't say 'Long time no see'.

SPEER. Why not?

WOLTERS. It's what you said when you got out.

SPEER. Did I really? Well, it hasn't been so long this time.

WOLTERS. It has been long enough.

SPEER. Now look.

A young MALE PUBLISHER *enters with a tray: full glasses of champagne, a bottle and a plate of bits.*

MALE PUBLISHER. Herr Siedler thought you might like something before it all goes.

SPEER. Thank you, yes.

MALE PUBLISHER (*picking up the edgy atmosphere*). You were . . . it was champagne . . . ?

WOLTERS. It was champagne.

The PUBLISHER *goes out.* SPEER *hands* WOLTERS *a glass.*

Well . . . to two old codgers and their memories.

They drink.

WOLTERS. From one old codger and his royalties.

Pause.

Of which I'm sure the vast proportion have been properly donated to the best of causes. It would never do for the great post-Nazi rent-a-penitent to profit from his crimes. Having resolved to walk into his dotage in a hairshirt, renouncing all the vanities and luxuries of life for locusts and wild honey.

SPEER (*gesturing to the feast*). So, a locust? or another spoonful of wild honey?

WOLTERS. Well, precisely.

SPEER. So is this why you came to see me? To draw my attention to this contradiction?

WOLTERS. No, of course not.

SPEER. Rudi, I didn't mention you because I thought it would be best. As an architect practising in the current atmosphere.

WOLTERS. You think I didn't like your wretched book because I wasn't in it?

Enter a young FEMALE PUBLISHER.

SPEER. If not, I apologise for the suggestion.

FEMALE PUBLISHER. Ah, Herr Speer, I've found you.

SPEER. Yes, I am having what is obviously \ a private conversation –

FEMALE PUBLISHER. There is . . . I have to tell you . . . there's a lot of people \ waiting for your signature –

SPEER (*sharply*). But still a moment if you please!

Slight pause.

FEMALE PUBLISHER (*put out by being snapped at*). Of course.

She turns and goes. SPEER *to* WOLTERS.

WOLTERS. Oh, don't worry. I'm not the first thing to be rubbed out of your past. And I doubt I'll be the last.

SPEER. I have said, I'm sorry.

WOLTERS. Though you were right in one respect. The reign of terror's hotting up again.

SPEER. The reign of terror?

WOLTERS. Having run out of all the various butchers of wherever, moving on to the so-called 'perpetrators from the desk'.

SPEER. Yes?

WOLTERS. Which is why I came to see you.

SPEER. Oh?

WOLTERS. The Chronicle.

SPEER. Yes, you wrote to me. I wrote back. There's a problem?

WOLTERS. Describe the situation as you see it.

SPEER (*slightly offended*). Rudi.

WOLTERS. All right. From 1940 I kept a chronicle of your activities. Of which there were four copies. Three are lost, the fourth I bury in my garden. In 1964 I dig it up, have it retyped, and two years later I hand this retyped version on to you. And like the splendid citizen you are you hand it over to the Federal Archives in Koblenz.

SPEER. Yes.

WOLTERS. However there is a British writer called David Irving \ who finds another copy –

SPEER. – who thinks that Hitler is a man much misunder-stood . . .

WOLTERS. – who points out that Hitler was an ordinary, walking, talking human being with grey hair, false teeth and an obsession with his bowels. As opposed that is to either Superman or Lucifer Incarnate.

SPEER. And he comes across another copy of the original. In some library?

WOLTERS. The Imperial War Museum . . .

SPEER. . . . and compares it to the retyped version in Koblenz . . .

WOLTERS. . . . and finds they're not the same. Because your old friend Rudi has been through the original, correcting style and grammar, and deleting one or two things that he felt were irrelevant or repetitive or just plain silly . . .

SPEER. Which is all understandable enough, hence my proposal that we send Koblenz our original, which if anybody wants to plough through they're quite welcome. After all, Irving has presumably ploughed through it all already.

WOLTERS. I see. You think that Irving read it all.

SPEER. I understand he's more than diligent.

WOLTERS. The London copy's incomplete. It's only 1943.

SPEER. So he gets to catch up on the rest in Germany. Rudi, I really don't see the problem.

WOLTERS. The problem isn't 1943. The problem's 1941.

Pause.

SPEER. Yes?

WOLTERS. Do you remember, when your father asked the Chief where the people who'd been dispossessed would go?

SPEER. Yes, I suppose so.

WOLTERS. To which the then official answer was that the plan was for them to go and live in garden suburbs.

SPEER. Yes.

WOLTERS. While as it fell out, actually, a lot of them would end up somewhere very different.

Slight pause.

SPEER. So? I was the General Inspector of Buildings. I had nothing to do with the evacuations.

WOLTERS. Not directly.

A sharp knock on the door.

SPEER. Yes, what?

The MALE PUBLISHER *is trying to get* SPEER *to come out.*

MALE PUBLISHER. Herr Speer, I know you're busy, but there is a considerable queue \ outside –

SPEER. I *know*. I will be with them *very shortly*.

WOLTERS. Natives getting restless.

SPEER. So?

WOLTERS. Minutes of meetings 1941. Attended by our people, Goebbels' people, and SS-Lieutenant-Colonel Adolf Eichmann. To plan the eviction and evacuation of nearly 80,000 persons from Berlin. I wonder, can you guess what race of persons these 'persons' might have been?

SPEER. And you cut this out.

WOLTERS. Yes I cut this out.

SPEER. Although far from silly or irrelevant.

WOLTERS. Yes.

SPEER. You know I didn't know of the evictions.

WOLTERS. I'm afraid you did. There's some notes, still
    happily in my possession, with an entry on I believe the
    20th of January 1941. 'Couple action on the Jew-flats with
    preparation for emergency quarters for persons' – rather
    different persons, obviously – 'made homeless through
    bomb damage'. All quite clearly in your writing.

SPEER. Well, of course, I knew that people were deported.
    As I have always said. I didn't know where they were
    going.

WOLTERS. No of course you didn't. That's the point. They
    were just another group of people, being shoved about.
    Along with soldiers, foreign workers, ordinary prisoners,
    prisoners of war, conscripted or evacuated, bombed out,
    picked up, taken in custody for the protection of, relocated,
    handled, processed, dealt with. In the chaos of a war which
    was already termed a war of national survival. It's only *now*
    it looks like what you claim it was: the first step on the road
    to what you 'should' and 'could' but didn't know was the
    Greatest Crime in Human History.

SPEER *shrugs at this sarcastic hyperbole.*

But *now* it all looks different. You know that Theo
Ganzenmüller wrote some note in 1942, confirming he'd
been able to provide some trains for the transportation of
some persons somewhere as requested. The kind of routine
memo we all wrote a hundred of a day. Unfortunately, the
somewhere was Treblinka.

SPEER. Well, yes, of course . . .

WOLTERS. But you, great National Scapegoat, you reverse it.
    It's remarkably ingenious. You flagellate yourself in
    hindsight actually to justify your actions at the time. Your
    sin is to have stood above the fray, to have kept your hands

clean, never to have known. And by this sleight of hand
your betraying him turns into him betraying you.

SPEER. Rudi, that's enough.

WOLTERS. So when did he stop living up to your grand ideal?
Well, by the bunker, obviously. So, when he gave you the
the Arms job? When you designed Germania? When you
joined the party? When you sat about and planned a better
world with me?

SPEER. You know, it's interesting, what you say about
betrayal. Because for all those years, whenever I felt lost, or
let down or abandoned or betrayed, whenever I was near to
losing faith in humankind, I'd tell myself: just think of Rudi
Wolters.

Pause.

But I suppose, we knew \ that it could never –

WOLTERS. Which is why I have to tell you what I really feel.
How could I lie to you? It would be as if I lied to me.

SPEER *looks at* WOLTERS, *with the stirring memory of
that sentiment.*

SPEER. Well at least, we must hope, it isn't lost for ever.

WOLTERS. What, your faith in humankind?

SPEER. Unlike the original version of the Chronicle. Which
should I think be lost forever.

WOLTERS. I'm sorry?

SPEER. As so much else has been. After all, it refers to matters
which aren't in the book. About which I knew nothing. So,
for the greater good.

WOLTERS. We should pursue the line of least resistance.

SPEER *looks askance.*

Oh, don't worry. The original will vanish without trace. As
if it never was. From your and everyone's domain.

SPEER *stands a moment. Then, suddenly, he turns and goes back out, almost bumping into the entering* MARGRET.

MARGRET. Albert, I have been sent to drag you \ back . . .

SPEER. I'm coming. Look who's here.

He goes out.

MARGRET. Rudi. How wonderful to see you.

WOLTERS. Margret.

They shake hands. She looks questioningly.

I have been talking to the Great Best-Seller.

MARGRET. When he returned, you know, it was to be the Modest Architect. Have you read the book?

WOLTERS. Oh, yes. Have you?

MARGRET. I read the bit about Eva Braun. He seems to have been quite taken with her. I always found her rather bossy and pretentious.

WOLTERS. Of course, he talked much more about you and your courtship in his letters to the children.

MARGRET. Yes. Hilde showed me. It was incredible. All these feelings which he had inside. From a man who virtually never said a word to me.

He offers her champagne. She declines.

I've been chatting with Klaus von Below. He's considering a book himself. But he's afraid, there was some incident. A young man came to see him about something dreadful that he'd witnessed. And of course there was nothing he could do.

WOLTERS. It was a war. And it was a quarter of a century ago.

MARGRET. Of course.

Slight pause.

You know, he's working on another book.

WOLTERS. Oh?

MARGRET. It's about his time in Spandau.

WOLTERS. Ah.

MARGRET. Some of it was lying on his desk. It was a description of a dream.

WOLTERS. He always said the Spandau dreams were quite agreeable.

MARGRET. Not this one.

WOLTERS *looks inquiringly at* MARGRET.

It begins with Albert in a factory. Someone – Hitler I presume – is coming for a great inspection. And although he's Minister of Armaments, he's sweeping up the floor.

WOLTERS. At Nuremberg, they made the surviving prisoners sweep up the gymnasium where they'd done the hangings.

MARGRET. Well, that would explain it. Then like you are in dreams he's in a car, and he's trying to get his arm into his jacket.

WOLTERS. Presumably, that's the jacket Hitler lent him when they met.

MARGRET. Of course. And then he's in a vast square, I suppose the great square that they planned for all those years, and Hitler's there as well, and asks his adjutants: where are the wreaths? And then Albert looks surprised, I would imagine, because the adjutant explains that nowadays 'he' lays wreaths all the time. And so he does, singing a kind of dreary plainsong chant, as on and on they come, wreath after wreath, piled ever higher, seemingly without end.

She's looking out towards the garden party.

And look. Look, still they come.

WOLTERS (*sensing she's talking about something else*). Excuse me?

MARGRET. He's still signing.

WOLTERS *turns out front.*

WOLTERS. Not for the last time. As his Spandau Diaries were to prove another publishing phenomenon.

But once again, there was no place for his indefatigable and yet absent 'friend'.

Those years in which I was his lifeline, and he was my life.

WOLTERS *goes.* MARGRET *out front.*

MARGRET. I'm sorry. I would like to talk about it, but I can't. I'm sure you understand.

You see, my fear is that sometime, somebody like you, with the best of good intentions, will ask me what I knew.

And I don't know which is worse. Having known about it . . . or the truth. That I knew nothing of what went on at all.

I am so sorry.

MARGRET *turns and goes out.*

2.5   A music auditorium in a University, Germany, early 1970s

The music auditorium has been taken over by a meeting that has had to move from a large hall – it is crushed and crowded and there's an improvised quality to the arrangements – the female student CHAIR *sits on a piano stool, there is no table in front of the guests* SPEER *and* SIEDLER, *no water jug or flowers, and the lectern is a music stand. There are* SECURITY MEN *among the* AUDIENCE.

CHAIR. Fellow students, fellow members of the University Historical Society, ladies and gentlemen. I must first of all apologise for the conditions. Which as everybody knows were brought about by the actions of people who prefer to shout down rather than to listen and discuss. We are grateful to the music faculty for loaning us their auditorium at such short notice. Well, at none at all.

Slight pause.

As you know our speaker this evening is the author of a noted and important autobiogaphy, about an unhappy period in our country's recent past. He is accompanied by his publisher, Herr Siedler. We are very grateful to them both for agreeing to proceed with this symposium under the circumstances. Herr Albert Speer.

SPEER *goes to the music stand. Applause and a little booing – the booing is booed back.*

SPEER (*adjusting his notes*). No, no.

Putting on his glasses.

Well, first of all I am very pleased to be speaking in a place dedicated to music. However, I must confess that I am here under somewhat false pretences. I have never been a speech-maker, and in fact there is a story illustrating this. On the occasion of his 50th birthday, I was pleased to hand over the first completed stage of the new Berlin to Hitler. For some days he had been announcing gleefully: 'A great event! Speer's going to make a speech!', and when he arrived he took his place expectantly. I took a deep breath, cleared my throat and spoke these exact words: 'My Führer. I herewith report the completion of the east-west axis. May the work speak for itself!'

It was of course a good joke. And I must admit my pleasure that he accepted it as such. 'You got me there, you rascal, Speer', he'd say. 'Two sentences indeed!' Still, he told me it was one of the best speeches he had ever heard.

We are detecting opposition in the room.

And of course I made many other speeches, including one at the Nuremberg trial, in my defence. But what I want to do tonight is to explain to you how I can speak of Hitler as a normal walking human being . . .

FIRST HECKLER. Normal?

SPEER. And how it was not in fact till Nuremberg that I realised that, yes, this superficially normal human being was in fact \ a man of quite –

SECOND HECKLER. No Nazis! Speer out *out*!

SPEER. But I detect that there is something which you want to say to me.

SECOND HECKLER. Speer *out*!

SIEDLER. No, no.

CHAIR. Herr Speer, we ask you to ignore this anti-democratic spectacle.

SPEER. It would I fear be undemocratic of itself to do so.

Pause. The FIRST HECKLER *helps out the* SECOND HECKLER.

Go on, go on.

FIRST HECKLER. When did you know about the killing of the Jews?

SPEER. What, as a systematic policy of elimination?

FIRST HECKLER. Yes of course.

SPEER. As I say, at Nuremberg.

Chuntering.

CHAIR. Please, Herr Speer, do you continue your prepared address.

SPEER. No, I am happy . . . as I say, I am not an orator. I will answer questions.

Pause. SPEER *returns to his seat.*

CHAIR. Well, in that case, may I ask . . . ah, yes.

Points to FIRST QUESTIONER.

FIRST QUESTIONER. Speaking of Nuremberg, Herr Speer –

AUDIENCE. Can't hear!

The FIRST QUESTIONER *is handed a microphone.*

FIRST QUESTIONER. Speaking of Nuremberg, may I ask about your work on the design of the party rallies there?

SPEER. What about them?

FIRST QUESTIONER. Did you feel that by providing such spectacular visual effects you were an important part of the Nazi propaganda machine?

SPEER. Well. At the time, I was a professional architect. My job was not to be concerned with political issues.

SECOND HECKLER. No, of course not!

CHAIR (*to* SECOND QUESTIONER). Yes, please.

SECOND QUESTIONER. 'Herr professor', when you joined the party, were you an anti-semite?

SPEER. No. As far as practising anti-semitism is concerned, or making anti-semitic remarks, my conscience is entirely clear. Nor, as it happens, was I a real professor.

SECOND QUESTIONER. But you were a real Nazi.

SPEER. I was a member of the National Socialist Party. And yes, I knew the party was anti-semitic, of course, and I also knew the Jews were leaving Germany.

FIRST HECKLER. And being murdered?

CHAIR. Please.

SPEER. I'm sorry, I thought she was asking about when I joined. When, like many – most I suspect – I assumed that antisemitism was a – vulgar incidental to the party programme.

SECOND HECKLER. Incidental!

SPEER. Which of course proved to be far from the case. But even later on, I knew the Jews were being evacuated, but I did not know they were being murdered as a systematic policy.

THIRD QUESTIONER. Herr Speer, you do understand why people find this hard to credit?

SPEER. I understand that people do. But it is nevertheless the case.

Slight pause.

The final solution was a secret from the German people.
And as one of them, it was a secret from me too.

There is a hostile atmsophere growing in the room.
SIEDLER *feels he needs to rescue.*

SIEDLER. Perhaps to clarify this point, it's worth asking how
it was that a person of your position in the German state
would not know this.

SPEER. Well, as I say, \ the policy was secret –

SIEDLER. As clearly you knew people who *did* know.

SPEER. The whole ethos of the Hitler state was about the will
of a single individual. Everyone was told: you need only be
concerned with your domain.

SIEDLER. And if you had known, and protested, what would
have happened?

Slight pause.

SPEER. Well, people were shot for less. For example, Hitler
had made clear to me that if I countermanded him, that that
would be treason, with the usual consequences.

SIEDLER. You are referring to your overruling Hitler's orders
to destroy German industry in the last months of the war?

SPEER. That's right.

FIRST QUESTIONER. So why weren't you executed, when
you told him?

SPEER. I'm sorry?

As the FIRST QUESTIONER *quotes,* SIEDLER *searches
for the right page.*

FIRST QUESTIONER. It's in your book. Here. 'I confessed
to him in a low voice, that I had not carried out any
demolitions but had actually prevented them. For a moment
his eyes filled with tears'.

SPEER (*to* SIELDER). Um, where . . .

FIRST QUESTIONER. It's just before you offer to stay with
   him in Berlin. Presumably to die \ along with him and Eva –

   SIEDLER *hands the book over to* SPEER *to read.* SPEER
   interrupts.

SPEER. Ah yes. 'Perhaps he sensed I didn't mean it'. It was of
   course a time of great emotion. But it is true, at that late
   stage, he did not fulfil his threat. In fact, as I recall, he told
   me: 'We will never speak of this again'.

FOURTH QUESTIONER. So did 'his eyes fill up with tears'
   when he watched the film of people he'd had hanged with
   piano wire on meathooks?

SPEER. No, this is a myth. Hitler did not watch films of
   anybody being executed. He was notoriously squeamish.

FIRST HECKLER. You said he did! He said it in an interview!

SPEER. I was misreported. It was after all an interview in
   Playboy magazine.

   Laughter.

   You may know, they have a fold-out section: misquotation
   of the month.

   Laughter.

SIEDLER. In fact, I could read out what you actually said \
   about this incident –

   Suddenly, another QUESTIONER, *with documents, marches
   to the stage.*

FIFTH QUESTIONER. Or instead you could read this.

   The CHAIR *and* SIEDLER *stand.*

SIEDLER. Um . . .

SPEER. What is that?

CHAIR (*precautionary*). Please, Guard . . .

SPEER (*stands*). No, let him be.

A SECURITY MAN *hovers as* SPEER *goes over to the*
FIFTH QUESTIONER.

FIFTH QUESTIONER. It is a speech, transcribed from
phonograph recordings, from the state archives at Koblenz.

SPEER. Yes?

The FIFTH QUESTIONER *holds his document out to*
SPEER.

FIFTH QUESTIONER. Read it.

The GUARD *puts his hand on the* FIFTH QUESTIONER*'s*
arm.

SPEER. What is this?

FIFTH QUESTIONER. Read it.

SECURITY MAN. Come along . . .

SPEER. No, no.

He reads, a little bemused.

'You will not doubt that the economic aspect \ presented
many great difficulties' –

FIFTH QUESTIONER. Further up.

SPEER. 'I want to speak now, in this most restricted circle,
about a matter which \ you, my party – '

FIFTH QUESTIONER. From *there*.

SPEER. 'The brief sentence "The Jews must be exterminated"
is easy to pronounce. But the demands on those who have
to put it into practice are the hardest and the most difficult
in the world'. Who is it?

FIFTH QUESTIONER. Himmler. Now read that.

SPEER. I, um . . . You will forgive me . . .

The FIFTH QUESTIONER *snatches his papers and goes*
to the CHAIR.

FIFTH QUESTIONER. All right, you read it.

CHAIR. No.

FIFTH QUESTIONER. 'To listen, to discuss'.

FIRST HECKLER. Read it!

SIEDLER. I'll read it.

He reads the passage pointed to.

'We, you see, were faced with the question 'What about the women and children?' And I decided, here too, to find an unequivocal solution. For I did not think that I was justified in exterminating – meaning kill or order to have killed – the men, but to leave their children to grow up to take revenge on our sons and grandchildren'.

Slight pause.

Well, of course, it's terrible. When was it?

FIFTH QUESTIONER. 6th of October 1943.

SPEER. I'm sorry, when?

FIFTH QUESTIONER. 6th of October 1943. A meeting of Gauleiters, and some others, at Posen Castle in the Warthegau.

SPEER *looks at him aghast.*

Yes. You were there.

He takes the transcript and finds the next bit he needs.

Later Himmler talks of war production. How people tried to stop them liquidating the Warsaw ghetto because of the war production there.

CHAIR. Now, please . . .

FIFTH QUESTIONER. Then he says this: 'Of course, this has nothing to do with party comrade Speer: it wasn't your doing. It is precisely this kind of so-called war production enterprise which party comrade Speer and I will clean out together over the next weeks. We will do this just as unsentimentally as all things must be done in the fifth year of the war: unsentimentally but from the bottom of our hearts'.

SPEER. I wasn't there.

CHAIR. Please, this is enough –

FIFTH QUESTIONER. You're saying you weren't *there*?

CHAIR. Guard, will you ask this man to leave.

FIFTH QUESTIONER. But Himmler says: 'it's not your doing'. You were *there*.

SPEER. I wasn't there. I was there at the meeting in the morning, but I wasn't there.

The SECURITY MAN *takes the* FIFTH QUESTIONER *by the arm.*

FIFTH QUESTIONER. Take note please, everyone!

SPEER. I must have left. I needed to consult . . .

SECOND QUESTIONER. Let him speak!

CHAIR. I must insist . . .

SIEDLER. Now, Albert, it's all right.

FIFTH QUESTIONER. Don't you understand? Himmler's saying, Speer is here.

A SECOND SECURITY MAN *comes up to help pull the* FIFTH QUESTIONER *out.*

CHAIR. Herr Speer, I must apologise . . .

FIFTH QUESTIONER (*as he goes*). It's the whole case, torn to shreds. He didn't know. But he *did* know. Himmler speaks to him. 'It's not your doing'. In the middle of a speech in which he says of course we all know don't we that we're murdering the Jews . . . It makes it crystal clear . . . he's lying as he lied at Nuremberg and he's lied for thirty years . . .

He's gone.

CHAIR. Herr Speer, I'm sorry. Everybody, please . . .

SIEDLER. Come on, now, Albert.

SPEER. I was not. I cannot recollect. I wasn't there.

2.6.1   A synagogue, Dusseldorf, mid-1970s

Bruckner's Fourth Symphony is playing in the backgroud. An older CASALIS *enters with Rabbi Rudolf* GEIS. *Both men wear skull-caps.*

CASALIS. I'm afraid I don't think that this is a good idea.

GEIS. So why \ are you –

CASALIS. It's what he wants.

GEIS. So he always gets what he wants?

CASALIS. What he thinks he wants.

GEIS. Why does he want to meet death camp survivors now?

CASALIS. Something has happened. Some exposure by an academic, accusing him of being at a meeting where Himmler openly discussed the killing of the Jews. I gather from his wife he's spent weeks in the Federal Archives, checking dates and times.

GEIS. He didn't come to you?

CASALIS. No. But he wrote about it.

GEIS. I'm sorry.

CASALIS. Why?

GEIS. I thought that you were close.

CASALIS. We were. But under rather different circumstances. It's difficult to go on knowing someone one has got to know quite deeply in a time of crisis.

GEIS. Ah, that would explain it.

CASALIS. What?

GEIS. Why, in his books, he hardly mentions you.

Pause.

CASALIS. Yes I noticed that. I think . . . I have decided . . . I don't mind.

Slight pause.

GEIS. I'm sorry. I'm behaving like a prosecutor.

CASALIS. And we know our job is not to judge, to probe or to interrogate.

GEIS. Speak for yourself. Would you be surprised if he had lied about – whatever?

CASALIS. Well, he lied to me. I think. But then all prisoners do. It's a way of hanging on to the little of themselves they're left with.

GEIS. That surprises me. From his books, it seems Herr Speer is in complete command.

CASALIS. By then.

GEIS. Was that your work?

CASALIS. He never lied about his inner life. Let's say, he built a path on which we could walk together for a while.

GEIS. Both figuratively and literally.

CASALIS. A path – a rhythm, or a discipline – on which when I had left he could proceed.

GEIS. To become a different man?

CASALIS. That, and his writing.

Slight pause.

GEIS. Yes. I know a brilliant man, completely organised and disciplined, a lover of the arts and all the higher things . . . and yet. Not only incapable of abstract thought, but also of romantic love. I often ask myself, what happened to him as a child.

CASALIS. Then you know Albert Speer.

GEIS. So was he at this meeting?

CASALIS. His case is that Himmler was notoriously short-sighted, that the room was dark, and that he couldn't have been there. Which rests on not being able to fly in to Hitler's east headquarters, so he had to go by road, and a gap in Hitler's calendar in which they could have met that evening.

GEIS. And does it sound convincing?

During this, SPEER *enters in his overcoat, carrying his hat.*

CASALIS. Rabbi, I have a fear. That the only way he could admit what he admitted was by denying what he has denied. I taught him to confront as much of what he knew as he could deal with and remain alive. That to save his life he had to sacrifice his soul.

SPEER. Herr Pastor.

CASALIS. Why, my dear Herr Speer.

GEIS (SPEER*'s head's uncovered*). Uh . . .

CASALIS. Oh yes, you need a skull-cap.

SPEER *goes to get a skull cap from the pile by the door.*

GEIS. In fact, your own hat is perfectly \ acceptable –

CASALIS *returning with skull-cap.*

SPEER. No, no, this will do.

As SPEER *puts on the skull-cap.*

CASALIS. This is Rabbi Geis.

SPEER *and* GEIS *shake hands.*

SPEER. I am very grateful.

GEIS. They'll be here directly.

SPEER. Isn't that the Bruckner Fourth?

GEIS. Yes, it's my assistant.

SPEER. We had them play it at the last concert of the Berlin Phil.

GEIS. As you say in your reminiscences.

SPEER. I'm complimented. And your synagogue survived everything?

GEIS. With an occasional judicious change of role.

SPEER. Ah, yes.

GEIS. In fact, it may change role again. Unhappily, what was the ghetto is now prime downtown real estate.

SPEER. Oh but you mustn't sell it. It's so beautiful.

GEIS. Yes. Like the romantic symphony.

Slight pause.

SPEER. What do you mean?

GEIS. I have a theory, that there is a risk, that people – sometimes people who have found it hard to find love in their real lives – seek beauty in great works of art not as a supplement to personal love but as a substitute. That somehow, they can feel – feel deeply, passionately, soulfully . . . but not directly. So they feel through art.

CASALIS (*fearful that* GEIS *may have gone too far*). I think . . .

GEIS *notices his assistant* DAVID, *in his late teens, appproaching from his office.*

GEIS. This is I fear true of my assistant.

DAVID. Herr Geis, your guests are here.

GEIS. David, this is Albert Speer.

SPEER. How do you do?

DAVID. I've read your books.

SPEER. I'm glad.

DAVID. I have a question.

SPEER. Please.

DAVID. What are you proudest of designing, as an architect?

GEIS *and* CASALIS *are relieved.*

SPEER. The piece I feel about most – deeply and most passionately is a chair. It was very simple, rather unobtrusive. But for me . . . complete.

Pause.

DAVID. A chair.

GEIS. We'll meet them in my office.

SPEER. Oh, can we not talk in here?

CASALIS. I think it would \ be better –

GEIS. If it's what you want.

> GEIS *raises a finger, to indicate to* DAVID *that he should wait a moment.*

> But first I must ask you seriously if this is really what you want. I must put it to you that there might be something fundamentally unhealthy about living so intensely in the past. I have read your books. I know that you are now confronting other accusations. But surely – now – it is time to face the future.

SPEER. You have heard about this meeting I am supposed to have attended.

CASALIS. Yes.

GEIS. Did you attend it?

SPEER. I have proved – to my own satisfaction – I did not.

GEIS. To 'your own satisfaction'.

SPEER. The timing is quite clear. I had to leave the meeting early, and I drove to Rastenberg and met with Hitler. I have affidavits proving where I was and who with and how long. I have proved, yes, that I wasn't there.

> *Pause.* GEIS *says nothing.*

> For what is the alternative? That I was there and I don't remember? That I blocked it out?

> *Slight pause.*

GEIS. As you say, you have your affidavits.

CASALIS. And now perhaps we ought \ to go and see –

SPEER. Rabbi. It has been nearly thirty years. Nobody could go on asserting his own guilt at full volume all that time and remain sincere. I wake with it, I spend my days with it, I dream of it. But what I say about it has inevitably grown

routine. And now that I have proved – to my own satisfaction, yes – my innocence of yet another charge . . . the
danger is that in considerable relief at that I say – well if
that's all right, then there's no guilt at all. So if you will
forgive me, sir, I need this meeting. Because I need to know.

CASALIS. What do you need to know?

SPEER. What it was like, to be on the receiving end of me.

(*To* DAVID). So will you bring them?

DAVID *goes out,* SPEER *moves away to look at the
synagogue.*

GEIS *speaks out front.*

GEIS. And of course it was very hard for him. One of the
women was from Prague, and had been first at
Theresiensdadt and then in Auschwitz where she'd been the
victim of experiments.

CASALIS *speaks out front.*

CASALIS. He told me, once, that on his way to work he could
see the crowds of people waiting for evacuation on the
platform of the Nikolassee railway station. But he'd never
speculated what would happen to them at the other end.
Well, now he knew.

GEIS. The other was in hiding, and had spent her time since
trying to find out how and where her parents, uncles,
cousins, husband and two children died.

CASALIS (*to* GEIS). My understanding is, that Hitler's
calendar wasn't an appointments book. It was a record of
everyone who met with him. And on the evening of
Himmler's speech, Speer's name isn't there.

2.6.2   Germany, late 1970s

The images of what was at the end are projected on the set. Vast, unmanagable, inescapable. The Dora sounds: the cement mixer and the saw. SPEER *walks through the images, forming weird shapes on his body and his face.*

SPEER. And so they told me what I'd turned away from.

> *Pause.*

> So, yes, of course. That is the question I must answer now.

> Not whether I was at a meeting. But whether, meeting or no meeting, I still knew.

> And you were bound to ask eventually. Everybody does. And it is always the same answer.

> Because if I knew, and if I *knew* I knew, then everything becomes a lie.

> What I said to Georges Casalis, what I wrote, what I told my children, what I tell myself. My life becomes a lie to me.

> And so I have always said. I should have known, I could have known, I didn't know. I turned away.

> *Pause.*

> Yes, that's right. Turned away.

> *Pause.*

> I'm sorry. I can never speak of this to you again.

> *He turns. It is his study.*

2.7.1   Speer's study in Heidelberg, late 1970s

MARGRET *enters.*

MARGRET. Albert, there's someone here to see you.

> SPEER *looks round.*

It's a woman. She claims she has an appointment.

SPEER. Um . . .

MARGRET. She's German speaking, with an English accent. She's clutching all your books and articles. She's obviously more than diligent.

SPEER. Ah. Yes.

MARGRET comes over to SPEER, *gives him a letter.*

MARGRET. Albert, do tidy yourself up. You look worse than you looked in Spandau.

MARGRET goes out. A knock.

SPEER. Come in.

The door opens. MRS WINTERINGHAM *is in her mid-to-late 30s, fair and attractive. She does indeed carry a small Speer library.* SPEER *glances at the letter to remind himself.*

Mrs – Winteringham?

MRS WINTERINGHAM. Herr Speer, I am so pleased to meet you.

She comes over to shake his hand. Some confusion with her books.

I'm sorry . . .

SPEER. Please sit down.

They sit.

You have an English name.

MRS WINTERINGHAM. My husband's British. I live there, you see.

SPEER. I have always admired the British.

MRS WINTERINGHAM. Yes, I know. In fact, Herr Speer, we've met before.

SPEER. We have?

MRS WINTERINGHAM. You signed one of my books for me.

SPEER. Ah, yes. And, when . . . ?

MRS WINTERINGHAM. Herr Speer, I'm very angry.

Slight pause.

SPEER. Oh?

MRS WINTERINGHAM. I have read your books, your articles and interviews, and other people's articles about you.

SPEER. Ah . . .

MRS WINTERINGHAM. And my response is – what gives them the right to carp and sneer at somebody like you?

SPEER *is thrown by this unexpected tack.*

Herr Speer, I think your prison diary is the best, and the most moving book I've ever read.

SPEER *demurs at this hyperbole.*

And of course you made mistakes. In stirring times. How could you not? But you *were* Germany's chief architect. You *did* stave off defeat against all odds, and save our industry from destruction at the end. You *did* serve twenty years in solitary confinement, and transform yourself, and come through to make a new career. And for people to insist on yet more penitence, yet more self-accusation . . . Oh, I think not, Herr Speer.

SPEER. You're very kind.

MRS WINTERINGHAM. I am not being 'kind'.

SPEER. Nevertheless . . .

MRS WINTERINGHAM. There is no nevertheless about it. You did these things. They were of value. And you did them on your own.

SPEER *stands.*

SPEER. Shall we take a walk? You can make your notes when you get back.

MRS WINTERINGHAM. My notes?

SPEER. You have not come to interview me?

MRS WINTERINGHAM. I have come to meet you.

SPEER (*gesturing to the books*). So . . .

MRS WINTERINGHAM. I'd hoped that you might sign my other books for me.

SPEER. Of course. When we return.

MRS WINTERINGHAM *smiles and stands.*

SPEER (*picking up the book he signed*). Please ask my wife to lend you some galoshes. I will be down directly.

MRS WINTERINGHAM *turns to go.* SPEER *reads his inscription in her book.*

SPEER. Your name is Trudi.

MRS WINTERINGHAM. Yes.

SPEER. Yes. I think – I do remember you.

He looks at her.

Do you like music, Mrs Winteringham?

MRS WINTERINGHAM. Oh, Herr Speer, I am Aquarius. I love things of beauty more than life itself.

She goes out.

2.7.2   Germany, 1980–81

SIEDLER *and* HILDE, *speaking separately out front.*

HILDE. Apparently it was the Spandau Diaries. They 'made her cry'.

SIEDLER. I saw Speer in 1980. He'd sent me the manuscript of his new book on the SS, which had considerable problems.

HILDE. My mother was naturally devastated. After everything she'd done for him.

SIEDLER. And then he said what he had said to me before: that sometimes a man needs another man in whom he can confide.

HILDE. What, did she know? He used to 'report absent' when he went to meet her.

SIEDLER. And then he took a snapshot from his wallet.

He said: 'I had to be in my 70s to have my first real erotic experience with a woman'.

HILDE. Of course she knew.

2.8.1   Bedroom, Park Court Hotel, London, 1 September 1981

SPEER *in his bedroom. There is wine in an ice-bucket. He telephones.*

SPEER. Hallo? This is room . . .

He checks his key.

516. This is to say that there will be . . .

Pause.

Ah. She's on her way.

He looks round the room, checks his appearance in the mirror. There's a knock at the door. He goes and admits MRS WINTERINGHAM.

MRS WINTERINGHAM. Hallo, darling.

SPEER. Hallo.

They kiss, passionately.

MRS WINTERINGHAM. It's sweltering. How was the BBC?

SPEER. Oh, fine. They thought I'd done the plans for Hitler's tomb at Linz.

MRS WINTERINGHAM. But that was Giesler.

Pleased that she knows this, SPEER *opens wine.*

SPEER. Yes. I had to improvise.

MRS WINTERINGHAM (*enjoying his chutzpah*). You told them you did *Linz*?

SPEER. I left it open. Do you want some wine?

MRS WINTERINGHAM (*mock shock*). Albert.

SPEER (*pouring wine*). Being the BBC, they couldn't resist pointing out all that remains of my work are the ruins of the stadium, two gatehouses now converted into lavatories and a row of streetlamps.

MRS WINTERINGHAM. Now, stop that.

She kisses him.

SPEER. They invited me to lunch. I said I had a previous engagement.

She takes a glass of wine, and drinks.

MRS WINTERINGHAM. It's wonderfully cold.

She kisses him again.

Well. Cheerio.

MRS WINTERINGHAM *knocks her drink back.*

Hey, I could have a shower, couldn't I?

SPEER. Of course you could.

Taking off her jacket.

MRS WINTERINGHAM. And this evening, Herr Speer, I wish to be escorted to the theatre.

SPEER. You know, in Spandau, I made a theatre in my mind. I would imagine purchasing the ticket, leaving my coat in the cloakroom, buying a programme, sitting down. And looking forward to the curtain rising, and \ the cool draft from the stage –

She takes over as she goes out.

MRS WINTERINGHAM (*taking over*).' – the cool draft from the stage, with its smell of glue, dust and papier mâché'. Yes, I know. It was your imagination!

SPEER *takes off his jacket, loosens his tie.*

SPEER (*to himself*). Yes. If you think about it.

The room has been growing dark and peculiar. SPEER feels strange.

It was that that got me through.

SPEER *stands. The transformation is beginning to take place.*

So what's this here?

2.8.2   The Mausoleum

SPEER *is looking through the smoke at a huge, emerging space; the grey expanse punctured by a line of lights stretching into the distance.*

SPEER. What's going on?

Pause.

SPEER. Is it . . . am I in a street?

A MAN *emerges from the darkness, throwing a huge shadow.*

SPEER. This is an air-raid?

The MAN *approaches, followed by other* MEN.

SPEER. Or else . . . torches? This is Nuremberg? Is this then? Is this me?

HITLER. No, Speer. It's me. And now.

HITLER *is in stormtrooper uniform.* HESS, SCHAUB, HANKE, *also in stormtrooper uniform, behind him. It's like a gangster raid.*

HITLER. As if you didn't know. So what have you been up to since I saw you last?

SPEER. What do you mean?

HITLER. As if I didn't know.

He turns and nods to the others, who swagger upstage into the darkness.

You've been trying to remake yourself. You have been trying to become a different man.

SPEER. What's this?

HITLER. Having been 'condemned, robbed of your liberty, tortured by the knowledge that you'd based your life upon a lie'.

SPEER. Oh, of course, the dreams.

HITLER. Having been 'intoxicated', 'blinded' by the power I granted you.

SPEER. The dream. The dream in which you know.

HITLER. How you nevertheless stood up heroically at the end, to save the last weak remnants of the German people. At risk of being taken off and shot of course! How you were not responsible for the conditions of your labourers but now I understand you are suddenly responsible for Linz! But as you say. The dream in which I know.

SPEER. I never said you'd have me shot.

HITLER. Oh no? What did you tell that pornographic magazine?

SPEER. I'm not sure I recall.

HITLER. 'My Führer . . . there is something I must say to you . . . ' 'What is it?' You be me.

SPEER. 'What is it?'

HITLER. And then you: 'My Führer, all these months, when I have been pledging my unfailing loyalty, I have been sabotaging everything you have commanded. When I said I stood unconditionally behind you, I was actually betraying you behind your back. When I said I'd never lie to you, I was actually lying at the time. And I didn't have the guts to tell you then, but I don't have the guts to live with my deceit and so now there's nothing you can do about it I'm confessing it to you. Oh, and if you like, I'll stay here in Berlin with you and we can die together!'

SPEER *says nothing.*

And what did I say, then? According to this fairy tale?

SPEER. 'We will never speak of this again'.

HITLER. Oh yes. And my eyes 'filled up with tears'. Whereas what actually occurred, on this momentous evening?

SPEER. I'm afraid I don't \ remember.

HITLER. I passed you in a corridor. I said 'Goodbye'. And that was that. But, oh no: 'My eyes filled up with tears'.

Pause.

Hm?

SPEER *says nothing.*

And the workers in the mountains. And your *shock*. And *pain*.

SPEER. In fact, I did my best \ to improve their conditions –

HITLER. Your shock and horror at my 'giving up' the German people.

SPEER. I didn't realise you could be so \ heedless of their fate –

HITLER. But most of all, the lie that after everything you didn't know.

Pause.

SPEER. It was true. I didn't know. As I have proved to my own satisfaction.

HITLER. *What*? *Still*?

SPEER *shrugs, confirming.*

Had I not always said that once the strong had been eliminated, all is lost and it is pointless trying to save the rest?

SPEER. Of course.

HITLER. That without its strongest elements, the German people would degrade into a feminised and weakened lumpen mass, as prey as Slav subhumans to the cholera of Bolshevism?

SPEER. Yes.

HITLER. That the Soviet state was a criminal conspiracy that would have to be destroyed, with implacable determination?

SPEER. You'd implied that, certainly.

HITLER. And does not the destruction of a state 'imply' the physical elimination of its functionaries, without mercy or consideration of the rules of war?

Slight pause.

And when I said – as I said repeatedly, and publicly, that if there was a war, it will lead inevitably to the annihilation of the racial source of Bolshevism, why couldn't you believe it? Why did you insist that anti-semitism was 'a vulgar incidental'? I said it – clearly, time and time again. I didn't say 'resettlement' or 'cleaning efforts'. I did not speak of 'special handling'. And yet you all insist that when I said the Jews must be destroyed, I only meant 'defeated'. That when I said 'eliminate' I didn't mean 'exterminate', I only meant 'exclude'. That when I said 'purge' and 'perish' and 'annihilate', it was of course a metaphor. Why was I cursed with never being taken literally? How could the world have been so blind? And how could you?

Slight pause.

But oh. 'I turned away'. As ever. Not your fault. Why not admit it? Why not confess it? Why not come clean now?

SPEER *says nothing.*

Hah?

SPEER *says nothing.*

All right, I'll tell you why. Speer, you present yourself as a man inspired by a great vision but who saw that vision trampled into dust. By me. Yet without me there was no vision and there was no man. Who made you, Speer? Who appointed you his architect? Who promoted you to be his armourer? Who inspired you to dream dreams you could never dream alone? You did what I required of you. You realised my vision. And if you are in a hall of faces then the face is mine.

HESS, HANKE *and* SCHAUB *come forward with wreaths.*

SPEER. You are laying wreaths.

SCHAUB. He lays them all the time.

HITLER *lays wreaths.*

SPEER. Who they are for?

HESS. They are for the best.

SPEER. The best are dead.

HANKE. The best are dead.

HITLER. And of course when I said our new Berlin was a mausoleum, you did not believe me either. 'The names of our Germanic fallen, carved on every stone.'

SPEER *looks in anguish at* HITLER. HITLER *hands wreath to* SPEER.

So then: be me.

SPEER. There is no need. I have been you ever since I met you.

HITLER. Yes.

SPEER. I thought my life began with you. But it ended with you.

HITLER. Yes.

SPEER. You were the nightmare. Always. Obviously.

HITLER. Yes.

SPEER. Your tomb was Linz. Mine was Germania.

> SPEER *looks back for the last time into the huge grey disappearing space. His eyes are full of tears.*

HITLER. Why are you crying?

SPEER. I am crying for myself. And the life I could have led if I'd been different from the start.

HITLER. Come, come.

SPEER. No.

HITLER. The best are dead.

SPEER. No.

HITLER. The dead are best.

SPEER. No.

HITLER. And now you can be best.

> *He looks at* SPEER.

> At last.

> HITLER *turns with his* MEN *and goes.* SPEER *is alone. His eyes are closed. But then looks back, to see a different group of people.* HILDE, GEIS, CASALIS, ANNEMARIE, MARGRET. *Maybe, behind them, the* JEWISH FAMILY *from the Nikolassee, and the* DORA WORKERS *from the mountains. He looks at them.*

SPEER. Not yet.

> Because, yes, I cannot admit what I have not admitted and remain alive.

> But if I did, I could die the man I might have been.

> *To 'us'.*

> Of course, it wasn't that 'I could have known'. That I was 'blind'.

Because, yes, one cannot look into a void. If I 'turned away', I knew.

I knew. I helped to build a boneyard.

Yes. I knew.

And now, at last, I need never speak nor think nor dream of any of these things again.

Darkness. We hear MRS WINTERINGHAM*'s voice, distraught.*

MRS WINTERINGHAM. Please, you must call an ambulance. There's a man, he must have had a stroke. Please hurry. I think he may be dead . . .

Light. SPEER*'s body lies there. Suddenly, massively,* HIMMLER*'s face projected on all the surfaces of the set.*

HIMMLER. And with this I want to finish. You are now informed, and you will keep the knowledge to yourselves. Later perhaps we can consider whether the German people should be told about this. But I think it is better that we – we together – carry for our people the responsibility – responsibility for an achievement, not just an idea . . . and then take the secret with us to our graves.

Darkness.

'Since I am not going to go down in architectural history for buildings, I might at least have defiantly won a place for myself with grandly conceived plans. Am I, too, lacking an original desire to give form to reality? In the passion to produce something out of myself? Was I, too, made creative only by Hitler?'

Albert Speer, *The Secret Diaries*

AFTERWORD

It was on the third day of rehearsal. Sitting round a huge table in the bowels of the National Theatre, actors about to play Hitler, Himmler, Eva Braun and the stage army of the Third Reich were debating the plausibility of Hitler's Minister of Armaments not knowing about what was happening to Jews and others in the slave-labour and death camps of the Nazi empire. Suddenly, the argument escalated. Albert Speer was Hitler's favourite. As his architect, he had been a vital part of the Nazi propaganda machine. As his armourer, he was responsible for millions of slave-workers kept in unspeakable conditions. He kept the war going for a year longer than it needed to, at the cost of untold suffering. Whatever he knew or didn't know, did Speer have a case worth presenting? Was it worth us doing a play about this man at all?

This was not the first time this question had come up. It had been central to the discussions I had had with the play's director Trevor Nunn during the development of the play. And for both of us there was a *déjà vu:* the same debate had raged around the production of a play I wrote about the rise of the National Front in 70s Britain (*Destiny*), which Nunn programmed for the Royal Shakespeare Company in 1976. By seeking to understand people with dreadful opinions, or people complicit in crimes resulting from those opinions, is the writer (or director or actor) inevitably tending to condone?

The first immediate, instinctive response in this case was that the play *Albert Speer* is based on a well-reviewed, highly regarded and massively successful biography by Gitta Sereny, whose moral credentials and dignity of purpose were questioned by no one. However, this argument falls apart when the material is transferred to the theatre. However passionate its author, a work of history has an essentially magisterial relationship with its readership. Like the French legal system, the medium invites sober consideration of the evidence, the balancing of arguments and the disinterested search for truth. Like a British courtroom, a play tends to the adversarial, demanding that the jury identify with one side. In this case, there is no sober summing up of the evidence, many of the prosecution witnesses are dead, and the accused is conducting his own defence. And however critical we may be of him and it, are we not – by the very act of presenting it – implying that he has a case? Or – even more insidiously – that his moral anguish can be set against the suffering for which he has been held responsible?

Further, we were aware that we were telling this story at a moment when the history of the second world war is a matter of acute and current political contest. As we rehearsed the play, another drama was being played out in the High Court of Justice. However unambiguous Mr Justice Gray's finding may have been, the David Irving trial reminded everyone how much of the darkest events of the second world war are subject to interpretation, how deep is the controversy about the aims and history of the holocaust, and how much of our knowledge of it is based on essentially circumstantial evidence.

And we are exploring the case for and against a leading Nazi at a time when the supposed effects of writing are subject to unprecedented scrutiny. Not only are works of fiction cited as inspiring if not causing real life crimes (the 'go thou and do likewise' theory of literary influence) but works of non-fiction are called to account for the harm or even distress they might cause. Following the publication of her 1998 book about the Mary Bell case, *Cries Unheard*, Gitta Sereny herself was accused by the parents of Mary's victims of 'bringing up all the bad memories'. From this understandable concern with the feelings of people involved in tragedies, it has proved a short step to the argument advanced by a reader protesting against the serialisation of Gordon Burns' book about Frederick and Rosemary West in *The Guardian* on the grounds of the 'suffering, despair and pain involved in the subject matter', not for the relatives of West's victims, but for everyone. And both Marcus Garvey's painting of and Diane Dubois' play about the continuing iconic influence of Myra Hindley were condemned on the grounds that it was inappropriate to treat of her in art at all.

And yet – of course – if the subject of evil was removed from the dramatic canon most of the great tragedies would disappear from the repertoire. From Clytemnestra and Oedipus via

Richard III, Macbeth and Othello to the gangsters, gunslingers and Godfathers of twentieth-century cinema, great drama has always been obsessed with killers, natural born and otherwise. If it was really true that the purpose of drama is to encourage its audiences to imitate the behaviour of its protagonists, then the medium has a great deal to answer for.

But, sadly, the opposite view – that the point of drama is precisely to discourage such behaviour by showing how it will inevitably get its come-uppance – doesn't really wash. 'Don't do this at home' is as misleading a description of what drama counsels us as 'go thou and do likewise'. The awful truth – and it is awful, in both senses of the word – is that the response most great drama asks of us is neither 'yes please' nor 'no thanks' but 'you too?'. Or, in the cold light of dawn, 'there but for the grace of God go I'.

When, understandably but sadly, the parents of Mary Bell's victims wrote in *The Sun* that 'Mary Bell is not worthy of consideration as a feeling, human being', they were letting the rest of us off the hook. The notion that there is a thing called evil which separates the wicked off from the rest of us is a comforting illusion. The uncomfortable truth is that to under-stand *does* involve recognition and even empathy. It does require seeing the world through the eyes of the wicked person, and thus finding those impulses and resentments and fears within ourselves that could – we have painfully to admit – drive us to commit dreadful acts under different circumstances.

Drama is a test-bed on which we can test and confront our darkest impulses under laboratory conditions; where we can experience the desires without having to confront the conse-quences. As Peter Brook writes in *The Empty Space*, 'in the theatre the slate is wiped clean all the time'. Drama enables us us to peer into the soul, not of the person who has driven his father out on to the heath, but the person who has wanted to.

But that's only the first shock. The second is that we enjoy the view. As critics from Aristotle onwards have noted, we don't just learn but take pleasure from seeing the representation of things that in real life we'd regard as disgusting or repellent. Indeed, the pleasure is the thing that allows us to confront these unbearable aspects of ourselves. This is why children like fictional forms whose familiarity is distanced by their location in the mythic past, the animal kingdom or outer space. And despite the wealth of all-too-human examples of monstrosity, adult audiences too demand villains from other worlds, different species and indeed beyond the grave.

Since the late nineteenth century, the assumption has been that the closer drama is to the lives of its audience, the more powerful and painful it will be. But the problem with looking in a mirror is that you see what the world sees. Look into a picture, and you may see what you have disguised.

Finally, because we see ourselves in him, the tragic villain commands our sympathy (indeed, the difference between the tragic and the melodramatic villain is quite precisely that). At the end of *Albert Speer* a dying man thinks he sees his past self approaching him through the mist but discovers that what is really inside him is not his own past but the terrible reality of a man he had once admired and loved. Looking at him confronting that truth I hope that the audience will look through that refraction back at itself. Albert Speer was subject to a Faustian temptation, fell for it, and spent the rest of his life creating a past with which he could deal. To be one of his many victims is – thank goodness – unimaginable for a well-fed first-world audience in the year 2000. To give in to personal ambition, to realise a moral and ideological error too late, and to spend the rest of your life making inadequate sense of that failure is all too recognisable.

As screenwriter Paul Schrader argued in defence of *Taxi Driver*, if writers stopped inventing criminals, 'we would still have psychopaths, but we wouldn't have art. We would still have Raskolnikovs but we wouldn't have *Crime and Punishment*'. If Gitta Sereny hadn't written her book about Albert Speer, his slave-workers would still have died, but we would be less able to understand why. For that reason alone, it seems to me worth taking the risk of putting his story on stage.

David Edgar

This is a revised version of an article published in The Observer, 30 April 2000

APPENDIX

Principal Characters

Below, Lt-Col Nicholas (Klaus) von   Hitler's adjutant 1937-45, and the man in Hitler's HQ closest to Speer. He and his wife Maria remained Speer's friends after Nuremberg. His memoirs were published in 1980.

Braun, Eva   Hitler's mistress from 1932 and, in the last days of their lives, his wife. A Bavarian girl of limited education, she was assistant to a photographer when Hitler met her. Hitler's chauffeur said 'She was the unhappiest woman in Germany. She spent most of her life waiting for Hitler'. Never allowed to appear in public with him, she was confined to his private life.

Casalis, Georges   A former member of the French Resistance, he was chosen for the post of Spandau prison chaplain because he was Protestant, spoke German, and was a man of impeccable morality and exceptional humanity. He stayed at Spandau for the first three years. After doing his PhD and working for several years in Nicaragua, he became curator of the Calvin Museum in Noyon. He died in 1987.

Ganzenmüller, Theodor   Young railway official, a protégé of Speer's, and suggested by him to Hitler in 1942 for position as head of the railways. He and Speer worked closely on rail transport for armaments to the front. He was implicated in arrangements to transport Jews to Treblinka and though brought to court, declared unfit to plead on health grounds.

Hanke, Karl   Secretary in Goebbels' ministry and Speer's patron. He offered Speer the job of redecorating his Grünewald villa. Hanke was Magda Goebbels' lover, for whom she wanted to leave her husband. Goebbels threatened to take the children away and Hitler forbade him. Speer mediated. Hanke resigned and entered the army, leaving in 1941 to become Gauleiter of Lower Silesia.

Hess, Rudolf   Deputy leader of the Nazi Party, he burned
with religious fervour for his leader. Hitler: 'With Hess every
conversation becomes an unbearably tormenting strain. He
always comes to me with unpleasant matters and won't leave
off'. He flew to Britain in May 1941 to persuade George VI to
dismiss Churchill, make peace with Hitler and align with
Germany against Russia. He was taken prisoner and remained
in custody until the Nuremberg Trials. Sentenced to life, he
lived to become Spandau's last prisoner, and was found hanged
there at the age of 93.

Himmler, Heinrich   Reich Leader of the SS from 1929, head
of all police from 1936, and in direct charge of the
extermination programme. 'Whether [Eastern] nations live in
prosperity or starve to death interests me only insofar as we
need them as slaves for our culture. Whether ten thousand
Russian females drop from exhaustion while digging an anti-
tank ditch or not interests me only insofar as the anti-tank ditch
for Germany is completed'. Arrested in May 1945, he took
cyanide before he could be interrogated.

Kempf, Annemarie (formerly Wittenberg)   A passionate
young Nazi, she was recruited by Speer from Goebbels'
'Gauleitung' at 17. Her husband Hans went missing in action
in Russia, 1944. After Speer was sentenced she worked on a
farm; later accepted a job in Bonn in order to campaign for his
early release; spent the rest of her life caring for disturbed
children, and remained Speer's friend till his death.

Schaub, Julius   Rose from Sergeant to SS General by 1945
without substantially changing his role as Hitler's Personal
Aide. Sent to the Berghof in April 1945 to burn Hitler's private
papers.

Tessenow, Heinrich   Philosopher architect under whom
Speer studied. Speer: 'I admired – no, I worshipped him,
but it never became a personal relationship in any way'. The
only architect who refused to participate in the redesign of
Berlin, he lost his chair at the Technische Hochschule, though
due to Speer's intervention kept a second chair at the Academy
of Arts.

Todt, Fritz   Head of construction for the Third Reich's Four Year Plan. He joined the Nazi party in 1922 and rose to be an SS colonel. Appointed inspector general of the German road system in 1933. He served as Reich Minister for Munitions, 1940-42. As creator of the Autobahn system, he was 'one of Germany's most influential men' and the world's principal user of concrete. He died in a mysterious accident in February 1942 and was succeeded as Minister for Armaments by Albert Speer.

Wolters, Rudolf   Speer's associate and helper throughout his life. Like Speer, his father was an architect; they met as students in Munich. Speer recruited him as part of the team redesigning Berlin; he went with Speer to the Ministry of Armaments; during Speer's imprisonment he remained his lifeline, taking charge of the family finances and processing the 25,000 letters he wrote from Spandau.

Apart from Speer and Hess, the other prisoners in Spandau were:

Dönitz, Karl   Commander of the German navy from 1943 and nominated by Hitler to succeed him. After Hitler's death, he became Head of State for seven days in May 1945. Sentenced at Nuremberg to 10 years' imprisonment, he was released in 1956.

Funk, Walther   The Third Reich's minister of economics from 1937 to 1945. Appointed President of the Reichsbank in 1939. Arrested and tried as one of the 22 major war criminals at Nuremberg, he was sentenced to life imprisonment, but released from Spandau on health grounds in 1957.

Neurath, Konstantin Freiherr von   Made Foreign Minister in von Papen's 1932 Cabinet and stayed on in Cabinet when Hitler became Chancellor. He was removed from the Ministry after protesting at Hitler's plans for conquest. Sentenced to 15 years at Nuremberg but released in 1954 on health grounds.

Raeder, Admiral Erich   Commander of the German navy from 1935 to 1943. When war came, his failure to stop the Allied convoys crossing the Atlantic infuriated Hitler, who forced his resignation and replaced him with Dönitz. Captured in Berlin in 1945, he was found guilty at Nuremberg and sentenced to life imprisonment. He appealed in vain for a death sentence, and was released in 1955.

Schirach, Baldur von   Head of Hitler Youth from 1933 to 1940, and Gauleiter of Vienna from 1940 to 1945, Schirach escaped capture at the end of the war and hid in the Austrian Tyrol, posing as a novelist. He was arrested and charged mainly for his administration of foreign workers and his treatment of Jews in Vienna. He was sentenced to twenty years' imprisonment.

Chronology of the Third Reich 1933–45

1933   National Socialist leader Adolf Hitler and former Chancellor von Papen agree on a coalition. President Hindenburg gives Hitler the Chancellorship. German parliament building burnt to the ground. Hitler is given emergency powers by presidential decree. Thousands put into camps by police and the SA (brownshirt stormtroopers). Dachau concentration camp opened. Enabling Law passed, giving special powers to the Chancellor (Hitler) for four years. Labour Unions dissolved. Law Against the Establishment of Parties makes Nazis the only legal party. All journalists registered and licensed to write. Hitler takes Germany out of the League of Nations. Speer meets Hitler for the first time.

1934   Night of the Long Knives. Hitler orders the killing of his enemies in the Nazi party. A law is issued legitimizing all the killings. Death of President Hindenburg. The office of President is abolished, Hitler supreme as Führer of the Third Reich.

1935   Treaty of Versailles disarmament clauses renounced by Hitler; universal conscription ordered. The first Nuremberg laws on Jews are announced in the official gazette. Further laws will be published each year. The Nazi swastika banner becomes the national flag. National Law of Citizenship: marriages between Aryans and Jews or Mischling (mixed race) forbidden.

1936   German troops re-enter the Rhineland. Spanish Civil War begins. Germany triumphs at the Olympic Games in Berlin, though medals won by black Americans, including four gold to Jesse Owens, cause embarrassment to the Nazis. Mussolini announces anti-Communist Axis with Germany.

1937   Speer's German pavilion faces the Soviet pavilion at the Paris World's Fair.

1938   Hitler marches into Austria, which ceases to exist. All laws of Germany, including racial laws are made to apply to Austria. All Jewish wealth to be registered. At a meeting in Munich, British PM, Neville Chamberlain agrees with Hitler, Mussolini, and Daladier that the Sudetenland should be annexed by Germany. In 'Crystal Night' pogrom throughout Germany more than 7,000 Jewish shops are looted, hundreds of synagogues burnt down, and 20,000 Jews arrested. All Jews are expelled from schools. Compulsory 'Aryanization' of all Jewish shops and firms.

1939   Germany occupies Bohemia and Moravia (Czechoslovakia) as 'Protectorates'. Confiscation of all Jewish valuables. Soviet-German non-aggression pact. German armies invade Poland and annexe Danzig. Britain and France declare war on Germany. Soviet Union invades Poland. Jews in Germany forbidden to be outdoors after 8pm in winter and 9pm in summer. Little military activity on the Western Front. Period of the 'Sitzkrieg' or phoney war.

1940   First deportation of Jews from Germany. German invasion of Denmark and Norway. German invasion of Netherlands, Belgium, Luxembourg and France. 'Fall of France' surrender signed at Compiègne. Hitler visits Paris. Battle of Britain.

1941   Germany occupies Bulgaria, Yugoslavia and Greece. Rudolf Hess flies to Britain on an unofficial peace mission 'Barbarossa': German invasion of Russia. Hitler issues the 'Commissar Order', legalising the killing of non-military Russians; no soldier who kills anyone in the specified categories can be held responsible. Gypsies and Jews are quickly added to the list. Millions of civilians, non-Jews as well as Jews, are killed. Göring orders Heydrich, chief of SS security police, to submit a draft for the achievement of the 'final solution to the Jewish problem'. 1.5 million Jews shot in the conquered Russian territories. Yellow star compulsory for Jews in Germany. General deportation of German Jews begins. Japan attacks Pearl Harbor. Germany declares war on USA. German troops falter 50 kilometres from Moscow, where the temperature falls below −40°c.

1942 'United Nations' conference in Washington: Britain, USA and Soviet Russia agree on no separate peace with Germany. Wannsee Conference formalises the 'Final Solution' (the extermination of the Jewish people). Death of Fritz Todt in an air accident. Speer succeeds him as Minister for Armaments. Hitler appoints a Commissioner General to organize the mass deportation of slave workers from the east. Over 3.5 million put to work in the first year. Deportation of 300,000 Jews from Warsaw ghetto, mostly to Treblinka, one of the four extermination camps. Mass gassings begin at Auschwitz. German troops enter Stalingrad. Germany now at its peak of conquered territory. Russian counter-attack at Stalingrad.

1943 Final surrender of Germans in Stalingrad. Germans and Italians surrender in North Africa. Soviet victory at Kursk. Germany now unable to wage offensive war in Russia. Mussolini overthrown and imprisoned in Italy. Allies land on Italian mainland; Italy surrenders. Italy declares war on Germany.

1944 Allies capture Rome. 'D-Day' Anglo-American landings in Normandy, France. Graf Claus Schenk von Stauffenberg tries and fails to assassinate Hitler. Paris retaken by Allies. Russians enter Rumania and Yugoslavia. 400,000 Hungarian Jews killed at Auschwitz, bringing total of gassings there to 1.2 million. Russians enter Hungary. Ardennes offensive – the last major German offensive action.

1945 Russians liberate Auschwitz. British cross Rhine to the north. Vienna taken by Russians. Anglo-American forces drive east. British liberate Bergen-Belsen. Berlin entered by first Soviet forces. Hitler commits suicide. Admiral Dönitz becomes Head of State for the last seven days of the Third Reich.